AN

UNSTABLE

CONTAINER

AN UNSTABLE CONTAINER

ESSAYS

JOHN LaPINE

DURHAM, NC

An Unstable Container
Copyright © 2025 by John LaPine

All rights reserved. No part of this publication may be reproduced or transmitted in any form or by any means without written permission from the copyright holders, except in the case of brief excerpts or quotes embedded in reviews, critical essays, or promotional materials where full credit is given to the copyright holder.

Library of Congress Cataloging-in-Publication Data

Names: LaPine, John, 1991- author.
Title: An unstable container : essays / John LaPine.
Description: Durham, NC : Bull City Press, 2025. Identifiers: LCCN 2024036019 (print) | LCCN 2024036020 (ebook) | ISBN 9781949344103 (paperback) | ISBN 9781949344585 (ebook)
Subjects: LCSH: LaPine, John, 1991- | Authors, American--21st century--Biography. | Gay people--United States--Identity. | LCGFT: Essays. | Autobiographies.
Classification: LCC PS3612.A64373 Z46 2025 (print) | LCC PS3612.A64373 (ebook) | DDC 814/.6--dc23/eng/20240829
LC record available at https://lccn.loc.gov/2024036019
LC ebook record available at https://lccn.loc.gov/2024036020

Published in the United States of America

Cover art: Anna Sovi
Book design: Jennifer Champagne

Published by
BULL CITY PRESS
1217 Odyssey Drive
Durham, NC 27713
www.BullCityPress.com

For M—'s father (1960–2024),
for Zelimkhan Bakaev (1992–2017), and
for anyone else who has ever felt scared
for being themselves.

TABLE OF CONTENTS

NSVs   1

Classics   29

On Alcohol   43

M—   63

An Unstable Container   87

Acknowledgments   109

About the Author   111

NSVs

Five minutes before English, Lauren tells our class she's got a trick.

"Did you know you can tell a gay person by their fingers?" she says. "My dad read it in a magazine. He's a doctor," she loves reminding us. Her dad reads lots of scientific journals; we hear this every day. "He's on the precipice of discovery," she says. The eighth-grade class crowds around her desk, bumping shoulders. I watch from my desk next to hers.

"Straight men have long ring fingers," she says. "And straight women have long index fingers." To demonstrate, she holds her long, white fingers together in front of us like picket fence planks adorned with silver rings. Even from my seat, it's obvious she's got the right ratios. "A person with inverted lengths is *queeeer*," she says, a hard *Q* with *EE* extra drawn out, making the word accusatory poison in her mouth. She turns her hand so everyone can see her perfect straightness.

As if hypnotized, each kid extends their hands in front of them, to learn their lengths. Twenty-four hands rise, and forty-eight eyes scrutinize. Who could miss a chance to spot the queer? My hand raises too, as if Lauren's compelling it, lifting it herself through telekinesis. She reaches across the aisle and grabs my wrist.

"Ha, gay hand," she says, jabbing a French-manicured fingernail into my palm.

"It's not," I say, tugging my arm back and shoving my hand into my denim pockets before anyone else can inspect it. The teacher walks in late, and we continue our analysis of Elie Wiesel's *Night*. But my focus all class is on my fingers, my inverted ratios. Lying my hand on my desk shielded behind my book, I try to peek at their lengths while the teacher calls students to read. When Ms. Davis calls on me to read, I don't know where we are.

■

Jon knows how hard it is for me to ask for help. As my roommate and best friend, he's seen me walk away from games of Frisbee when I tossed the disc too short because I felt too embarrassed to keep playing. He knows whenever I feel embarrassed, my short fuse means I give up early, sparing myself a hot, flushed face. He's heard stories of me throwing childhood tantrums in gym class.

So when I ask him, "Will you teach me how to throw?" I wonder what he thinks. That he'll be the next victim of my sports-induced vitriol, that I'll leave him alone in the yard after a few failed tosses.

"How to throw a ball?" Jon says. Incredulity alights on his face; his dark eyebrows rise and a smile tugs at his lip. There aren't a lot of twenty-four-year-old men who don't know how to throw a ball. It's a rite of passage for many men much younger than me. I try not to read amusement in Jon's face; I don't want my inability to amuse him. A graduate student should know how to throw a ball, I think.

"I never really learned how to throw," I admit. Perhaps the only person in the world I'd ask, Jon and I have grown together since we'd met. We'd spent hours together grocery shopping, thrifting, antiquing. We'd grown so close, friends had started referring to us as "The Jons." Our latest venture was working out together—spotting each other on the weight bench, planning morning runs together, keeping each other's diets honest, and cooking for each other.

NSVs

"I'll teach you," Jon says. His voice reassures. High school hockey helped him develop his coordination and stamina; I didn't play any sports. My biological father and I never played catch. In fact, I won't ever meet him—Dennis—the man who gave me half my genes; he will die next year from a post-stroke heart condition at age sixty-two.

Jon steps out through the sliding glass door and I follow, crushing fragrant grass beneath our feet. I walk backward from him until I decide I've reached the right distance to throw. Jon shoos me back further, gesturing with his long arms. I shuffle more. His features start to blur. Soon, all I can see is his dark hair, the shadow of his nose. I wonder if my pitch will reach him from here. I fear it won't.

We take our pair of brand-new mitts to the backyard, Jon with ball in hand. It's a warm spring day. We rent a small, one-story house with a large backyard on the outskirts of our rural city in Michigan's Upper Peninsula. In the backyard, stones encircle a charred fire pit we dug ourselves. A small forest of various trees marks the property line—thin white birches, gray-barked oaks, sticky white pines, white ashes, and sugar maples. Our tall, unmown grass feeds and houses dozens of varieties of insects: mosquitoes, clouds of gnats, red aphids, black flies, deer flies, deer ticks, American burying beetles, dragonflies, and on tepid nights, luna moths and lightning bugs. Often deer bed down in the forest, even right outside our bedroom windows.

■

I spend the rest of the school day examining my fingers. I hold them together flat on the lunch table, ignoring my cafeteria pepperoni pizza rectangle. I hold them out in front of me in art class, caked in clay. Still gay. The top of my ring finger barely reaches the cuticle on my index. On both hands. No matter how I angle them, they are so gay. By sixth period, the fingers still haven't changed, and I ride the bus sitting on them, pressing them into the gray leather seats.

By eighth grade, I had already wondered if I was gay; my "crushes" on girls felt forced, and I was more interested in my guy friends. But it took until the finger ratio to seal it in my mind. I knew correlation was not causation; it was my attraction to men—not my finger ratio—that determined my sexual orientation. Still, being gay had left its biological fingerprints all over my body, and my long index finger was proof.

To keep my secret, I make a mental note to avoid ring sizings, joining hands in prayer, séance, or any other activity that might make my fingers visible. For the rest of my life, I decide, I will never get my palms read. My heart and health lines will remain encrypted, concealing hints of my future. I'll need to take precaution when waving, high-fiving, shaking hands. At the time, I wanted to slice my fingers off; they shed my secrets like skin cells, their lengths a whisper you might hear if tuned to the right frequency. I start holding my fingers curled, hands balled into fists or even just holding each other, in case someone might look at them and interpret the runes.

■

"Ready?" Jon says. He throws the ball before I respond. It rotates slightly as air catches the stitches; it speeds toward

NSVs

me. It's a great, technical pitch. I stretch out my arm, my fingers pulling the tough leather mitt open, but the ball falls several feet away into the carpet of grass below. I shrug off the miss and grab the grass-stained ball. I expect embarrassment to crowd my mind and shut me down. But it doesn't; I feel comfortable being incapable with Jon.

A patient teacher, he'd become my workout partner, and had helped my form in weightlifting and squatting, held my feet during sit-ups, critiqued my jogging stance. "Chest out, shoulders back," he'd say as we trucked along wooded trails near our house. "Shorter steps up hills. Keep up," he'd huff. We'd seen each other covered in sweat, armpits and backs damp, struggling to stay upright during the final mile. We'd yelled "Spot!" at each other when the barbell grew too heavy, our arms shaking and threatening to give out. I learned failure through Jon. Or, we learned it through each other.

"Don't be afraid to run for it," he says, his baritone voice drowning out chickadee birdsong in the backyard.

"You either," I say. It's a joke: neither of us expect my first pitch to be a zinger. I turn the ball around in my ungloved hand, rubbing the cowhide exterior along my palm, feeling the red stitches protruding from its face, the smooth surface marred by raised sutures. I touch the laces with my long index finger, gripping the orb tight, preparing for the pitch.

■

By sixth grade, I'd become aware of my body, its mass, the space it takes up. I fit differently into tight classroom desks, belly pressing fiberboard. In gym, I lagged behind my peers, walking the last laps during warm-ups. I stop running and start spending more time indoors. During one clothes-shopping trip, I ask my mom if she knows why I am so big.

"You're not big. You're husky," she says, then changes the topic. "Are you excited to see your aunts and uncles?" We walk through the activewear section and search for a new swimsuit for summer. Huskiness runs in this side of my family; my aunts and uncles have been watching their weights for years. Each year, a new system. Sometimes it works, like when my uncle dropped forty pounds after a stomach surgery. My mom warned me about his appearance before his annual visit to our family cabin.

"He's going to look very different," she said. And she was right; his wrist- and cheekbones stood exposed, excess skin sagging from his neck and arms like a thin sheet, graying hair wirier than I remembered. But the system never works for good in this family; the next year, he would gain nearly all that weight back. I haven't seen him look that small since.

This year, I need a new swimsuit because I outgrew last year's, but none of the bright-colored polyester trunks appeal to me. I let Mom pick out a fluorescent blue pair.

"Looks fine," I tell her. But I know I won't wear it; I am too self-conscious of my growing body to swim in the lake, to let my family see me shirtless, rolls folding across my belly, my chest puffy and soft. Despite the lake's blue allure, I would not swim, for fear of exposing my bloated stomach and skin carved by stretch marks to my closest family members.

I had become aware of the changes of puberty as well. Hair sprouted from my forearms and legs, darker each day, and I started wearing longer sleeves and pants to cover the embarrassing growth. The hairs crept down my bicep, dandelion stems on the soft brown mound of my arm. I plucked them out each night by hand, blood dots pooling in moonlight, but every morning I'd find more, and wear only shirts with long sleeves, and sit in the back of the classroom and pull hair out when the teacher turned away.

"Want to try them on?" Mom asks, flipping a pair of trunks around so I can see the design.

"No," I say.

"You don't like the color?" she asks, fingering a red pair, but she knows blue is my favorite. "Do you want a different color, babe? Do you want a different design?"

"Let's just go," I say. "Please." Trying on the swimsuit would expose my body, my hairy legs, to her. I was nervous about the responsibilities my changing body would bring. Would other kids notice my hairy arms? Would that mean I needed to start dating? And how does dating work? How do you know when to kiss? Who to kiss? I didn't feel like a man, and I feared being treated like one.

I dare to throw the ball. I toss it underhand by instinct, my first misstep. Throwing underhand gives me more control over my own body; it has less strength, but I can predict where the ball will travel. It drifts across the yard. Compared to Jon's pitch, it's a snail. He lurches forward, mitt open, and steps hard on one foot to catch the lob. He readjusts himself upright and laughs; he wanted a real throw, the classic overhand pitch you'd see in televised baseball games. I want that pitch too, but the cruise control of my brain doesn't even consider an overhand toss. My body has never made that motion. Instinct says the underhand is safer.

"Try it like this," he says, and pitches the ball back to me. Watching his body, his motion is fluid; his long arm rotates up, then his back leg pops up like he's in the middle of a passionate kiss. The ball leaves his hand and sails through the air; it spins like a globe, showing off each side, each stitch— the Wilson logo black against white cowhide—on its way to my side of the yard.

I stretch my mitt, leather flared out, but the ball flies out of reach, soaring way above my head and diving to the earth, a rotund chickadee nesting in the grass with a thump. I've failed my first pitch, and both catches.

The words "throw like a girl" hum in my ear, and I fight the intrusive and misogynistic thought. I'd heard it hundreds of times, from peers, films, books, television, teachers, friends, even my own mother. "I run like a girl," she has said about herself. Or, "It'll make me scream like a girl." Maybe the thought was theirs once, but today it is mine alone. The stereotype, like all stereotypes, is toxic; plenty of women can throw better than me, and I know this. They're on professional teams; they're Olympians. They train their whole lives to throw precisely like girls; they repeat the motion ten thousand times. I wish I could throw like those women.

Still, I wonder if my aversion to sports was somehow borne through my sexuality. Maybe faulty hand-eye coordination and daddy issues are comorbid. Maybe exposure to increased levels of estrogen in the womb affects an embryo's brain, how we develop, training us to love men, shaping not only our fingers, but also our ability to slapshot or slam dunk. But, of course gay athletes have succeeded in every sport. The 2016 Olympics in Rio de Janeiro boasted the highest number of openly LGBTQ+ athletes;

NSVs

sixty-four out of 10,444. LGBTQ+ athletes participated in boxing, basketball, swimming, volleyball, soccer, rugby, field hockey, beach volleyball, handball, high jump, discus, badminton, kayak whitewater slalom, canoeing, judo, pole vault, taekwondo, road cycling, javelin, track and field, race walk, diving, equestrian, rowing, gymnastics, and the eight-hundred-meter run.

I want to group us together—myself with these athletes—because we are in the same group. Look what we've done, I want to say. Only, I have not achieved these things; they have. In 2016, LGBTQ+ athletes represented 0.6 percent of the competitors, and their successes—the fact that they've "made it"—means it's not impossible for a *queeeer* to compete alongside anyone else. If I have any inability, it is not my sexuality; it is mine alone.

I pluck the ball from the grass. In my hand, it feels like a round explosive; I'm afraid to hold it too long in case it detonates and takes half my right arm with it. I imagine shrapnel of cork and woven yarn embedding in my skull.

■

Scientists and researchers have studied the biological, measurable, quantifiable differences between heterosexual and homosexual people. Evidence from a 2003 study suggested homosexuals' hair whorls in a counterclockwise direction, whereas heterosexual hair whorls clockwise, supposed evidence of perhaps a "natural" way to be, a "right" and a "wrong" direction, visually and visibly betraying a secret of thousands of queer-identifying people worldwide. However, a 2009 study of one hundred homosexual and one hundred heterosexual men found no correlation between sexual orientation and direction of hair swirl.

This same 2009 study, however, did support an earlier correlation between birth order and homosexuality; the more older brothers a man has, the higher chance he identifies as homosexual later in his life. The hypothesis: a woman's body sees a male baby as a foreign and masculine threat, and produces more estrogen to counteract the object, a habit it continues as more male bodies form in her womb, resulting in gay men with several elder brothers. But endocrinology is complicated, and we cannot determine the degree to which our brief time in the womb affects sexual orientation later in life, and how much is determined after birth, or if those are even the right questions to ask. And I wonder what it means, that our queer bodies are shaped in this queer way. Does it dispel the idea that "sexuality is a choice?"

I have two older brothers—one step-brother, one half brother—but I am my mother's only son. At times, I've wondered if my father Dennis's absence was a catalyst to my homosexuality. If I knew my real father, perhaps I wouldn't be gay, I've thought. If my father and mother still loved each other, maybe I would be straight. But I also recognize the faulty and inexorable human tendency for clear, black-and-white answers. Does it matter whether nature, nurture, or some combination of both? Is it easier to sleep when we can draw a straight line between cause and effect, even if the two have never been linked?

■

For years, I let my hair grow long and curly because I was afraid to cut it. In this way, I let my peers' imaginary reactions control me. I feared their response—*any* response—to getting my hair cut. I wasn't afraid that my haircut would look bad; I was afraid of anything that drew attention to myself. So, I didn't cut my hair. I didn't want anyone to notice me changing; I wanted to be a constant. Reliable and invariable. I wanted to be a sure thing, a sign that maybe not everything is destined to change. That not everything will leave us. That maybe some things can stay gold forever. For me, this was my hair.

I let it grow throughout high school and college. Teachers would ask me to sweep my long, black curls out of my face. Classmates sitting behind me took joy in pulling it and letting it spring back to my scalp, or sticking pens into my hair, where they'd catch and hang for hours. One classmate asked if she could cut a lock and save it; I let her. My hair became iconic. It haloed my head like a helmet.

Around this time, I started getting confused for a woman. I'd be at the local Shopko, facing the shelves, when an employee would say, "Excuse me, ma'am." Or I'd be out to eat with my mom, and the waitress would say, "What can I get for you ladies?"

"You may have just offended my son," my mom would sometimes say. Other times, I would speak, and their faces would redden at my masculine voice. Sometimes neither of us said anything. But the misgendering almost always embarrassed the misgenderer more than me. I did feel a little offended, but mostly I was confused. I'd started to sprout a thin, soft mustache—another feature I was afraid to cut, so I let it grow for too many years. In my mirror, my face was not particularly feminine. Or, my mustache was so feminine, they thought I was a woman with a mustache. From behind, my long hair made it easy to see a Black woman with large hips and luscious curls shopping for Sour Patch Kids, rather than the seventeen-year-old male hiding behind a huge afro, trying to avoid being noticed.

■

It's my turn to throw again. I feel the ball in my ungloved hand, run my bare brown fingers over the laces, picking away at a string. For good luck, I think. I let go of my idea of a good pitch, swinging my arm back and releasing the ball at the peak of the arc. My shoulder aches and rolls, protesting the unfamiliar movement. The ball pops out of my palm, way too high—higher than the roof of our home—then falls short, hitting the ground several feet in front of Jon like a meteor. Jon chuckles again, and I want to believe he's laughing with me, not at me. But I know how ridiculous I must look, trying so hard to toss a baseball twenty-five feet, my face so serious and focused, my limbs flailing to mimic his pitch, then failing. My deltoid twitches like a strobe light, every nerve in my shoulder bristling.

"Think of your arm like a trebuchet," Jon instructs. I think about the piece of machinery, its heavy, wooden brick of an arm, and I wonder what mechanism makes it a perfect thrower. How does it know how to launch a projectile? Where does it get its leverage? How does it know the exact trajectory, how speed and angle combine to achieve a pitch so precise? What does it know that I do not? I imagine my arm a beam, all wood, my joints as rusty metal. The ball is a stone in the sling of my arm, and I channel medieval warfare when I hurl the ball. *Trebuchet, trebuchet.*

NSVs

■

During an all-dorm mixer, a room of fifty college freshmen and I drink putrid cherry punch in a cookie-cutter dormitory lobby. It's only 5:00 p.m. but night seeps through the windows this time of year, the windows like black holes, absorbing fluorescent light. I came to the mixer to meet new people, future friends, perhaps to find someone with shared interests. I sit on uncomfortable, tacky furniture that feels like upholstered cardboard while a bowl of candy travels around the room to reward each person who participates, saying their name and major, and why they're in college.

When the bowl arrives at me, I jump into my introduction. I say I study English.

"I hoped to study words, how they work. Their gravity," I say. "Their magic. Their ability to bring anyone anywhere, to describe anything. Words matter," I say. "I believe in them, and their power." Then I take a Reese's Peanut Butter Cup. Impressed with my own composure while speaking in public, I pass the bowl and run through what I've just said over and over in my mind. I sounded confident, I think. Not a downer. Mature, even intelligent. Friend material. I'm so proud, I don't hear anyone else introduce themselves.

Then, we break into small groups for an activity, and a resident adviser groups me with two other boys, each outfitted in Adidas, each hat backward. They look like clones—the same square jaws, the same blue eyes, as cookie-cutter as the lobby. We are handed a list of twelve celebrities— Mother Theresa, Michael Jordan, Steve Jobs, Thomas Edison, Abraham Lincoln—we're told they are all on a boat that will sink unless we throw five of them overboard. Our assignment is to determine who to throw to save the rest; it's an experiment in ethics.

In our small groups, we reintroduce ourselves.

"I'm TJ, here for business management," says one. "I'm gonna own a business like my dad."

"Hospitality management," says the other, Rick, dip of tobacco in his lip. "I wanna own a resort." He spits into a Gatorade bottle. I reintroduce myself to the boys. When I start speaking, they share a glance. They mirror each other's body language, sitting slouched, legs apart.

"You talk like a girl," says TJ, and I can feel blood rising, hot in my face. They notice this too. I could not help but feel slighted, and they knew this. I was not out of the closet. Not to these boys, not to any friends. I was hardly out to myself—for years, I held off from labeling myself, holding to the hope that maybe I was bisexual. At least then, I could *appear* straight. I'm not sure what they perceived in me that announced nonheteronormativity. But they rooted it out and attacked.

"You a queer?" asks Rick, pursed lips spitting brown into his bottle again. "You a sissy?"

"No," I lie. I don't want to answer, but I do. I don't want to engage; I want to finish the activity and go back to my dorm. I don't know why I stay, and I don't know why I answer. The rest of the room chitters around us. People meet new friends and swap contact information. They laugh about drowning Gandhi over Rosa Parks. I sit in uncomfortable silence, trying to conjure words to let me escape this interaction; the words don't come, so I stand up to throw away my candy wrapper.

"Ha, you even walk like a girl," says one of the boys. I'm not sure what offends me about their observation. Women

NSVs

are beautiful when they talk and walk. Perhaps it's my fragile masculinity that feels wounded—*not* the fact that I apparently perform the feminine gender role, but that I do not fit the masculine one. Not that a feminine cadence or saunter carries inherently negative traits, but that I was outside the prescribed binary.

They wouldn't jeer a woman for walking or talking "like a girl," but when a male adopts feminine characteristics, he fractures the expected binary. Back in my dorm, I bury my face in my pillow and fall asleep. Still, I resolve that week to sound more masculine, to un-lisp my esses. In classes, I drop my voice an octave. I walk less with my hips and more like a board, to make sure I don't sway. For some reason, I change myself for those boys—I intentionally do not say men here. They weren't. I don't know how I was before them, and I don't know if I can go back.

In late high school, I visited our family doctor for a check-up. Between fifth and ninth grades, my shirt size went from a youth large to a large to an extra-extra-large. At home, I was too afraid to step on the scale; at the doctor's office, I had no choice. I took off my shoes and stepped up on the frigid platform. A nurse slid the weight bar to a number; it clinked into a notch. I've mentally blocked that number, but it must have read almost two-fifty. That number must be recorded in a file somewhere in their office. At five feet nine, it meant "morbidly obese," about seventy pounds above a "normal" weight. This was me at my largest. In photos from this time, I look large, cheeks round, chins multiple. Most of my facial expressions in the photos are mock pain, or silly grimaces, eyes crossed or mouth agape, feigning happiness. I rarely took a serious or smiling photograph at this age, opting for "goofy" instead. I thought if I looked serious, then my problems would be serious. So, instead, I'd look silly, and my problems would be silly.

The nurse sat me down, and, after taking my vitals, listening to my heart, and recording my temperature, told me the doctor would be in shortly. The doctor, a middle-aged woman, brown-haired, brown-eyed, with cat's-eye glasses and a gold cross necklace dangling from her pale neck like a pendulum. She asked me the usual questions. How have I been feeling? Do I drink? How many in a week? Do I smoke? Do drugs? Not even marijuana? Am I sexually active? How often?

When I came out to her, her cat eyes didn't look up from her clipboard, but she scribbled it down with her yellow pencil. My medical record now says "MSM," or "man who has sex with men." My homosexuality lives alongside my heaviest weight in a file somewhere in their offices.

She told me, for my weight, height, and age, my blood sugar was too high, and I was at risk for "prediabetes," a serious condition, but reversible with diet and exercise. My mother had already been diagnosed with Type 2, and I would be next, the doctor warned, if I didn't change.

"And if you want to be healthy," she said, "you better choose to be straight." She told me the health risks of homosexuality—increased chance of contracting HIV, an increased rate of prostate cancer. "Children need both parents, a mom and a dad." The word "choose" made no sense; I couldn't control my attraction to men. There was nothing

NSVs

conscious, no choice to be made, and besides, why couldn't I be a mom? I often cursed my queerness, praying at nights that I would wake up straight, because life might be easier. Not just for health benefits. I wouldn't need to adopt or grow a baby in a test tube. No one could call me *faggot*, or *queer*, and I wouldn't need to come out; I could fit in. If I were straight, everything would be seamless, perfect, aligned.

■

My trebuchet is short again, and Jon runs to get it. Three throws, and not a single successful one. Three strikes. I want to yell "Yer outta here" to myself. I want to give up. But we'd only been out for five minutes. Quitting now would be more embarrassing, somehow.

"Try planting your back foot when you throw," Jon says. "You can get more force behind your pitch." He demonstrates the motion, swinging his arm back, rotating his shoulder, then kicking up his back leg. I picture my leg like a spring, and try to mimic his movements, my limbs acting as counterweights.

"And make sure you follow through," he says.

Jon retrieves the ball and pitches it back. It launches from his bare hand, right toward where I'm standing. I could catch it. But I don't start chasing soon enough. Instead, I stumble backward toward it late and it flies over my head. I pick it out of the lawn with my left hand. I think about a catapult as I drop my right arm behind my hip like loose rope. My shoulder tenses and I lift my arm back and above my head, and slingshot the ball toward Jon's open mitt.

With Jon as a workout partner and roommate, we kept each other accountable; we'd wake the other up at dawn to jog, reminded each other daily to lift or do push-ups. Soon, my body could run three miles at a time. Jon could lift more than me, and faster. He counted to ten before I got to six. But I caught up. When he jumped ahead, I caught up again. We were tethered together; we knew we could do better. On the weight bench, he counted reps and spotted, helped me learn skull crushers for my triceps, bicycle kicks for abdominals, squats for my quadriceps, calves, and glutes. Until then, I'd resigned myself to "husky," as if big bones were something genetic. Fate. Predestined.

■

In another version of this story, I have "nightmares" about gaining weight back.

In the true version of the story—I've gained some weight back. I wish I could say I wasn't self-conscious, but I am. Many days, I wish I were still in the body that wrote the rest of this essay. In a way, it's hypocritical, writing about how much the number on the scale doesn't matter, but still fantasizing about weight loss. And I'm trying to be okay with that.

I've entered my thirties, my sleep's a mess, I drink too much. My body and the number on the scale have changed, and I feel it. I feel my body protesting itself in a new way; not sore muscles but chronically achy from inactivity. For the first time in my life, I've regained weight. I remember being the kind of person who enjoyed exercise, but the new story is that I haven't broken a sweat in months. I remember when I enjoyed the soreness after a workout, that good hurt. These days, I'm struggling to find motivation, and to be that person I once was. I know the melody but I've forgotten the words.

I used to be the kind of person who believed words could take a reader anywhere; now I'm wondering if "anywhere" is a necessarily desirable location. The metaphors for how I feel remain elusive.

And I'm learning that "changing" oneself doesn't necessarily mean reverting to exactly the way things used to be. By the time we've committed to changing, we look around and realize we're in new locations. We've moved across the country, then back again. We've encountered new traumas, and all of this makes true reversion impossible.

I think about myself as a ball of yellow clay, and "change" is like wrapping it in a layer of blue clay. Trauma is the green that will inevitably be left behind when you try to pick away that blue layer. Green becomes a part of our journeys. And I'm trying to be okay with that, no matter how difficult.

In September 2017, scientists at Stanford University claimed they had taught artificial intelligence how to determine if a person was gay or straight based on facial structure alone. Researchers said gay men were more likely to have a narrower jaw and longer noses; gay women had larger jaws. The AI successfully identified gay men with 81 percent accuracy, and gay women about 71 percent of the time. The researchers pulled photos and self-reported sexual orientations from online dating profiles; the algorithm studied 14,000 faces. When LGBTQ+ civil rights groups GLAAD and HRC decried the study as both junk science and "reckless," "a weapon," researchers responded by saying they only developed the technology as a warning sign. They accused the "well-meaning lawyers" of trying to debunk good science but warned that their findings, if correct, "should be urgently addressed by technology companies, policymakers, and the public."

Internet commenters grew incensed, imagining a future in which automated robots could hunt down homosexuals by facial analysis alone, a video camera strapped to a motorized killbot that might exterminate our people. It's a scary—if unlikely—future. However, with the publication of this study and the development of this algorithm, it is increasingly likely. All it takes is one person with the will, the means, the technology. We now know it's not impossible.

Gay men are hunted and arrested and imprisoned in several countries today. In February 2017, sources reported the Chechen government held over one hundred gay men in secret prisons—what human rights advocates have called concentration camps. Ramzan Kadyrov, the Head of the Chechen Republic, claims there are no gay people in Chechnya. Chechen police and military officers invite men on dates, record their conversations, then blackmail the men with those recordings; their phones are searched for explicit, incriminating messages and photos. Police have encouraged parents to perform "honor killings" if they suspect their children are gay. Family members have turned in their own gay sons and brothers to the police for tarnishing family names. The journalist who broke the story has gone into hiding.

In August 2017, a pop singer named Zelimkhan Bakaev left his home in Moscow to attend his sister's wedding in Chechnya. He never made it to the celebration. Bakaev was never publicly out, but never married. In late September, two videos of Bakaev emerged on YouTube. In one twenty-eight-0second video, he dances near a couch and smokes from a hookah; his mother has noted several strange facts about the video, including the Chechen architecture, his sloppy haircut, and his weight loss. She believes he was forced to film the videos, or that the videos depict a body double; he had not been in contact with his family. Human rights advocates feared he'd been kidnapped and tortured; his family suspected he was murdered. In 2023, *The Advocate* reported that Kadyrov had shaken hands with Bakaev, and, upon learning of his sexual orientation, had personally ordered his torture and murder, dumping the body at the family home and instructing them to "bury him like a dog."

In October 2017, Egyptian police arrested sixty-five people who attended a Mashrou' Leila concert in Cairo after images emerged on social media of a rainbow flag raised in the crowd. The lead singer of the Beirut-based band is openly gay. Dozens of the arrested have been put on trial, and the band has been banned from the country for its "abnormal art." Detainees are subjected to anal probes, what Human Rights Watch says amounts to "torture." We don't have to wait for the automated killbots; the threat of being hunted is already here. Our own faces betray us, and I don't know which mask I should wear.

■

Some days, I hear my stepfather's voice come from my mouth. When I spend the day alone cleaning the house, I'm reminded of his days off; I remember coming home to the scent of lemon Lysol and freshly vacuumed carpet. Now, my roommates come home to the scent of Lysol and an out-of-season candle, Holly Berry in the spring and Apple Pie Spice in July. My stepfather and I share no blood, but as I grow older, our non-genetic bond pulls stronger, his impact on my psyche made manifest.

But then there are aspects of me I do not recognize in him, parts that are not my mother, and I wonder how much of me comes from Dennis, my biological father, the man I never met. When my temper flares, is that him? When I got detention at school for punching Chris D. in his glasses, bloodying his face for calling me King Kong, was it him? My mother said she didn't raise me to act like that. Did Dennis? When I feel the urge to tattoo my body, to pay a man to stick me with ink and needles, is that him? When I drop a man after two dates, is that my father? And my inability to throw this baseball—is it his muscles in my arms? His nearsightedness shaping my eyes? His large teeth rotting in my jaw? His clogged pores in my nose? Are his hands writing this essay? I want to take responsibility for my own actions, but the question of nature versus nurture still plucks at our brains—mine, and, by extension, his—how much do we share with our parents, even when they're absent? How much of us comes from their absences, the negative spaces where they're meant to be?

■

I spent years dreading writing this. I dreaded trying to make this make sense on paper like it does in my head. But people are complicated and thoughts are complicated, and knowing that is a simple kind of mercy. But it is more than the scale. I want to write about complicated ideas, but all stories need

NSVs

an ending that makes sense, and suddenly I'm no longer the person I was on the page, not just physically, but creatively, and maybe spiritually.

I'd like to say that this story has a happy ending.

I'd like to say I'm a weight-loss success story, that I kept posting pictures to social media to collect my congratulations every six months as I got fitter and fitter. I'd like to say I'm buff now and regularly post shirtless selfies.

I'd like to say I found fitness for life, that I made the "lifestyle changes" required to never have to worry about my weight or fitness, the number or my size.

And I'd like to say I've learned something about body acceptance since then, that I no longer feel bad looking in the mirror. But the truth is that I'm more self-conscious than ever about my body. It's hard to read a more optimistic, skinnier, perhaps more naive version of myself.

When I say I want this story to have a happy ending, what I mean is that I feel bad writing and publishing and thinking thoughts that might be fatphobic. Who does it serve to write an essay about weight loss, and the struggles of being big "again?"

I still struggle and feel bad. And I feel bad about feeling bad.

I want this to be nuanced. I want to write about how we shun "diet culture" while still congratulating others for embarking on and participating in "fitness journeys." Weight-loss communities celebrate nonscale victories—NSVs. These are moments in your life when you realize you've lost weight aside from the number on the scale. In another version of this essay, I would list them, but in retrospect, they each came back to the image of wearing smaller clothing sizes, or tightening one's belt, and those "victories" are hardly divorced from the scale.

I want people to read this and feel connection, not alienation. I wanted to preserve how I felt in the moment, but I also no longer feel this way, so editing this has felt impossible for years.

It's hard to find the language to describe this. I've "slipped," but that implies loss of progress. I've "let myself go," but that implies lack of control. I've "backslid," "failed," "messed up." I'm "worse."

I want to reclaim the language of regaining weight. I've let myself go and I feel freer because of it. I've slipped and survived the fall.

■

Now that I'm fitter, I'm focusing on my muscles, on becoming stronger. Muscle weighs more than fat, so I'm no longer trying to lose weight, but to gain it. I'm not trying to be the smallest; I want to be the strongest because I'm afraid I can't afford to be weak. Sometimes men like me get detained by governments; sometimes we are attacked by boys like the ones from college who told me I walk like a girl. Sometimes the attacks are physical. I need to know how to hold my own. I want to be able to save myself. I want to learn how to swing a bat.

Jon whips the ball back. I catch it in my mitt with a satisfying thump. The velocity surprises me, and the ball hits bone, a metacarpal where my finger meets my palm, the impact bruising through my mitt. I shake my hand and roll my wrist, eight small bones cracking like robin's eggs. The soreness in my back creeps along like vine tendrils. Lactic acid sours my cells; I roll my shoulder.

"Put your fingers along the laces," Jon advises, demonstrating a peace sign with his fingers. "Let them guide your hand as the ball rolls."

I try to remember all the advice Jon's given on how my body needs to move, to look, to feel, to throw properly. Leg planted, kicking up for force, follow through, watch how I, fingers on laces, let it roll, look right here, arm a trebuchet, loose like rope, follow through, follow through, and don't be afraid to run. I try another pitch; it sails faster this time. Jon's eyes widen and shift as they track the moving target—my fastest pitch yet—and he snatches it out of the air.

"There ya go," he says. It feels good to impress him. More than that, it feels good to accomplish the task we set out to do. I make a few good pitches, and more good catches. For a minute, we hit a rhythm, and neither of us drop the ball. When the sun sets, a brisk chill cools the spring air. We throw the ball back and forth a few more times, until the sun slumps below the tree line, shadows lengthening like outstretched legs. We won't have a chance to throw the ball again that year. We will get new jobs. We will move across town together to a house with a postage-stamp yard and be too busy for ball, and the mitts will sit in our new basement the entire year, as if frozen behind museum glass. But the soreness in my palm will last for days, an invisible bruise. I'll thumb the warmth beneath my skin. Today, I made my body listen. I feel it taking new form.

Through the magic of imaging technology, researchers estimate the brain makes decisions up to eleven seconds before the body enacts them. I wonder what this means about fate. One day, I'll die; I didn't used to care, but now it's all I think about as I try to fall asleep. I might go missing. I might swerve across the center line. I might be dancing in a nightclub in Orlando. Or my death might be slow. My cells might forget how to kill themselves; I might find them in a lump. My children might watch me unlearn their names. All I know is: it will happen. W. S. Merwin wrote that, once a year, we live through the anniversary of our deaths without realizing, and that thought makes my heart beat slower. Somehow, it gives all this more meaning. So I hold my own hands, lay them both across my belly, and become conscious of my decelerating pulse.

Lately, I've been aware of the fingerprints I leave around my home: the invisible oils anointing my pens and books, my mouse and keyboard, my cutting boards and knives, the light switch in my bedroom, my steering wheel, every doorknob, and perhaps, somewhere, in rural Michigan, that ball. But let them know me as I lived. Let them find my dirty dishes on my writing desk, my half-drunk coffee with half-and-half, my half-read books, a hard drive half full of half-written poetry. Let them dust for the imprint of lips on my spoons. Check the bite marks I leave in the last piece of fruit on my nightstand. Study everything I've touched. Let them know me from my teeth.

CLASSICS

Since 1955, the words "Where men cut men's hair" have adorned the window of Classics Barbershop, frosted into the glass of a single-room parlor tucked away by autumn red oak trees, and when I pull open the screen door and the bell peals above my head, I realize the shop will live up to this promise of professional masculinity—where men cut men's hair; the owner of Classics has outfitted the walls with dozens of retro ads for pomades, tonics, and aftershaves— Suavecito, Wildroot, Shiner Gold, Murray's—sepia signs advertising boys' "little league" cuts, waxed and combed, for seventy-five cents, but today the barber charges twelve bucks a head. One ad on the wall reads *"Ask your barber for a tip; stop dandruff with Kreml!"* Another in the reflection of the wall-sized mirror depicts a buxom sex symbol in a tight black one-piece bathing suit who allegedly *"Won't date a man who doesn't use AeroShave."* Pennants for pro sports teams hang from the ceiling: the Tigers, the Red Wings, even the Packers, an out-of-state favorite, emblematic across Michigan's Upper Peninsula. The chemical scent of alcoholic aftershave and creamy pomade saturate the place, as does the hum of electric clippers. The black-and-white tile and the red antique leather chair call back to the year the shop opened, a time many believe was simpler.

"How's it goin'?" the barber addresses me with a nod and a hint of a Fargo-style Upper Midwest accent I'd recently trained myself out of. "Mmgood," I say and nod back, trying to mimic his body language. The barber is a tall man with a good haircut—buzzed, uniform sides, impeccable fade, the crown styled and gelled into a swoop. Dark ink penetrates his thick forearms in the shape of mermaids, anchors, and life preservers. A hula dancer. A nautical star. He rotates a man with shaggy white hair in the antique chair; the barber stands still as his nimble fingers clip and comb. The barber's kind eyes frame a wide nose, and when he stops concentrating on the head he's working on, his face defaults to a smile. He wears a silver watch—black face, no numbers—pressed gray slacks, dark gray shirt, cheap black foam shoes. His teeth are all white and straight.

I find a seat against the wall in line behind three other men, plus one family of four—mother, daughter, son, and father. Mom holds the boy by his tiny pink hands, his blue Nikes separated from the floor, swinging him like a smoking thurible on a chain. The black plastic chair pretends to be comfortable; I pretend to be comfortable, rolling the knots in my shoulder against the molded polypropylene seat.

In each corner of the room, red, white, and blue barber's poles stand erect; they once had a job, spiraling to entice customers to enter. Now, they stand guard inside, quiet, retired sentinels. The flat-screen in the corner is tuned to Fox Sports. Another customer opens the screen door.

"Got you a coffee," says the regular, letting the screen door slam behind him. "Figured you might need it."

"Thanks," says the barber. "I don't usually drink coffee this late in the day, but I'm gonna need it today." The barber sets it down without taking a drink. He has spent the morning spilling blond and brunette locks onto the checkerboard floor.

"Do you want me to razor the back?" he asks the man with white hair. He coaxes some lotion onto the back of the man's neck with his index and middle fingers, reaches behind himself without looking to grab a straight razor off the counter, and, in one motion, brings the blade back to the flesh. I watch the blade shimmer in the mirror as the barber

Classics

carves a line across the man's spine, scraping away the stubble, then wiping with an off-white towel. He finishes with a proud flourish and a foamy wipe like he's signing his name.

On the TV, a woman with golden hair says something about Tony Romo's career, his ballooning salary or his fractured rib. I'm unsure; I tune out because I don't talk sports and I can't understand the appeal. I never played sports as a child; no basketball, baseball, football, soccer, or hockey. I was too sore a loser to play. In Boy Scouts, I threw a tantrum after taking second place in a foot race. A second- or third-place ribbon was a sour insult—look at this kid who can't even win. Even worse was the "Twelfth Place" ribbon from track and field day, a participation trophy the color of pea soup. As an elementary schooler, I somehow struck out in T-ball. A classmate yelled, "Three strikes, you're out"; I took one last, fourth swing before smashing the plastic bat on the ground and suffering through another meeting with the principal. "I'm your princi-*pal*," he said. We had a meeting whenever I lost my temper. We met too often.

The white-haired man in the chair says, "My wife has been driving me crazy. She never puts her dishes in the sink." He sounds like he's looking for validation; how dare she?

The barber says, "I've been learning to pick my battles with mine."

"Happy wife, happy life," says the man in the chair with a shrug.

"You want the aftershave?" the barber asks. He strokes the comb through milky tresses one more time like a paintbrush.

"Nah," says the man. "Even though I really like your aftershave. It smells so good. Actually, yeah, give me that aftershave." The barber wets his hands and massages the man's scalp, rubbing his fingertips over the skin he'd just smoothed. The man stands up and pays fifteen dollars, and the barber punches the digits into his old-school register with a *ding*. The customer refuses his change with a wave of his palm, and the barber stashes the tip back in the register.

"I love you, man," says the customer as he walks out the door. Man. The last word assures an understanding. It's platonic.

"Love you too, man," says the barber. He doesn't sweep up.

In the corner, the mother stands up; she's got other errands today. She's trusting her husband with the kids. She trusts him to get this right.

"Remember," she says to her husband, "no buzz cut. I want him to have *some* hair." The screen door jangles shut when she leaves. Her daughter watches her mother leave, then hoists herself up onto her father's knee and kicks her feet back and forth while her brother picks an insect off the floor and squats to examine it.

The next customer steps up to the red leather, a young man with shaggy, jet-black hair.

"What are you looking for today?" the barber asks. He shakes off the tarp and wraps it around the young man.

"This, but shorter. Shorter sides, long top, okay?" he says. The barber tells the man he must not be from around here. It's a statement, not a question. No, says the man, he's from South Korea. He's studying in the cold north for one semester. Six weeks in but he hasn't seen our snow yet. He just got out of the military, a mandatory engagement in his country, he says.

"I was never stationed out there," says the barber. "I was in Iraq. That's where I got these tapes," he says, without

Classics

motioning. I look to the corner to see a pile of VHS tapes under the flat-screen. They're labeled as old MMA fights from the early 2000s. "What did you do?" probes the barber. I check my watch; I've got a department meeting on campus in forty minutes.

"Ground to air," says the man in the chair. By the wall, the blond boy and his sister have gotten into an argument about who deserves the lap. The sister stays rooted, leaving her brother in tears. His father tousles his hair and lifts him onto the other knee. The girl flashes a jealous look. The boy keeps crying.

"I cut hair," says the barber. "In the Air Force," he clarifies. His dad and grandfather owned this shop before he did, he says, addressing not just the man but the whole shop, looking up from the neck in the chair and briefly into my eyes. But the barber never imagined himself following his father's career. He grew up cleaning this place, sweeping the floors and wiping the counters. When he took over ownership, he remodeled; his father claims the shop was busier back in the day, and calls the artifacts on the walls "junk." The barber navigates a pair of clippers all around an ear, not watching where the hair will fall; it drops to his shoe. With a spray bottle, he *kshk, kshk, kshk, kshk,* wets the man's head into a slick skullcap. "We should require service too," he says again to the shop, "we" meaning the United States. "It would straighten a lot of people out." He takes some hair into his wide white hand and trims it with his scissors. He looks up again. He's looking for a response.

From back against the wall, I say, "No way, they'd eat me alive." I wonder if he's had this conversation before. My mind flits back to the last man I slept with—a former Air Force private turned prison guard turned high school principal. We met at his hotel, where we watched *Dragon Ball Z* in bed, then spent an hour exploring each other.

He told me, "For some reason, people think it's hot that I'm a principal," and I didn't have the restraint to resist saying, yeah that's kind of hot. He called me "Jake." I told him my name didn't really matter.

The barber holds up a mirror to show off his work to the young man.

"Looks great," says the young man. It's a military cut, high and tight and short all around.

It's the blond boy's turn; he's still in tears from his fight with his sister. Dad leads him to the chair, and she follows, arching her neck around the barber to get a better view. Hands folded behind her back, she stands on her toes and peers around the red leather chair. The barber places a booster seat over the chair's arms and sits the boy down on the throne, a stuffed bear who might topple over if bumped.

The boy's father instructs. "Shorter—but not shaved—or his mother will kill me." The barber fires up the clippers, their droning hum drowning out the TV anchors. He steers his clippers between the sobs, cutting the boy's fine hair into a clean comb over. It's a classic, alright: a modern day Beaver Cleaver, wholesome and American like Tony Romo and the US Air Force. Meanwhile, his sister has snatched her father's phone, captivated by a YouTube video.

"Look how handsome you are," says the barber, admiring his own art. He brushes the blond hair to the floor with a boar's-hair brush and unwraps the boy. "Do you want to save some hair?" the barber asks the dad.

Classics

"I dunno," he says. His voice wobbles, as if standing on chubby, newborn legs.

"Some women like to do it."

"Whatever you want," says the dad. From a drawer, the barber produces a card—a "My First Haircut" certificate of bravery, despite the teddy-bear prince's tantrum. The barber searches the chair and floor for the perfect piece of hair. He finds it on the chair's arm—pale, blondish, still intact—and tapes it to the card. The boy's cheeks are still salty and damp, but, somehow—somehow—he's survived.

When it's time for my cut, the barber nods me over. He drapes the tarp over my chest and wraps paper around my neck like a collar. His warm fingers press against my nape, and my mind flits back to the last man who touched me there, how his hand on my neck seemed to draw our mouths together. The way the fresh stubble on his neck rubbed my hand raw.

"I hope his mom is happy," the barber tells the room. "You a Packers fan?" he asks as his foot pumps a pedal that raises me up in the chair.

"Nah," I say. I don't tell him I hardly know the rules. The hydraulic motion bumps me up an inch at a time until I'm suspended in air.

"What cut are you looking for?" he asks.

"Uh, something high and tight?" I say, more like a question.

"You don't want that," he laughs. "That's a jarhead haircut." In the mirror, my face flushes. My armpits grow damp with embarrassment.

"Well," I tell the barber, "You're the expert. What do you think?"

"You want short? How about two inches?" he says. I can't picture my curly hair two inches tall, and the barber will end up buzzing it all off anyway. He starts the clippers and pulls them across my temple.

"Man," he says, "yesterday, we had four crying kids in here. Right at the end of the day too," he says. He's addressing the whole shop again—teddy-bear boy, his sister, their father still waiting for his wife to return, plus two new patrons—locals by the look of their Packers baseball caps, scruffy faces, and flannel apparel—who have entered since the boy's haircut began. Anything for conversation. No one seems to bite. "Four crying kids at the end of the day," he repeats. Fox Sports switches over to the Detroit Lions, the underdog team, even here in Michigan.

"Ndamukong Suh hasn't done much this year," the barber says. I recall what I know about the Lions player—first, he's a Lions player. Second, I watched him in an infamous game against the Packers a few Thanksgivings before; while I ate pumpkin pie and Reddi-Wip with my mother, he stomped another player in the head. The stomp appeared intentional, a lift-and-step with his muscular thigh that would crush any skull without a helmet. Even my mother, a woman with a Lions tattoo over her heart, couldn't defend the violence. ESPN anchors played the four-and-a-half second clip over and over throughout the holiday weekend, trying to analyze Suh's intent. The most naive say he slipped, in desperate disbelief that one man could do that to another on live television. Suh claims not to have seen the man underfoot, calling the stomp a misplaced kick toward a ball that wasn't there, but not long after the Thanksgiving incident, Suh did it again; he stomped another player. The NFL would fine him over $200,000 for aggressive, dirty plays in his first four years on the field. The barber buzzes my sideburns.

"Suh's pretty violent," I resolve to say. Neutral. Knowledgeable. Enough.

"I used to stick up for him," says the barber. He strikes my neck with the guardless clippers over and over as if tempering a blade on an anvil. I remember my roommate and his chunk of missing ear from a middle school haircut. Suddenly, I'm feeling vulnerable despite the daylight, and the next words come out of my lips before I realize it's happening.

"Me too," I lie. "I liked him until he went and did it again." Luckily, our conversation stagnates; the sound of clippers festers. I sense the barber shuffling around for another conversation topic. The slow news cycle means the Fox reporter will fill two minutes between commercials with a clip of pop singer Justin Bieber visiting with the Pittsburgh Steelers.

"I hate that," the barber sighs. He pushes the chair, which spins on its oiled pedestal, while he stands still with the blade; he lets my head move around his clippers.

"Hate what?" I ask. I assume he means filler news spots.

"Teams that associate with Justin Bieber. That guy's a fag," he says. I swallow my words while my heart presses through the skin on my chest. I feel my face get warm again as I search the room for any indication that anyone else feels outrage at the casual usage of a homophobic slur. But the two Packers hats are speaking with each other, and the father is busy resolving a dispute about which kid gets to play Angry Birds on his iPhone. For me, the word hangs in the air like smog. I try not to breathe, for fear of taking it into my lungs, and I'm suddenly aware of the straight razor scraping the hair standing up on my neck.

As the barber finishes my cut, the blond boy's mother appears in the window. The barber holds the razor steady against my neck. In the mirror, I watch him watch her. She opens the door and it jingles behind her. She lifts up her son and turns him around like a gem in her hands. She brushes yellow hairs from his brow and examines his fresh comb-over.

"I just want to say," she says, "he looks awesome. He is so handsome. I was worried you'd cut it all off." Happy wife, happy life?

"Thanks," he says. "I try." It's a stab at humility.

But in the mirror, the barber's kind eyes don't widen; he knows the work he does—and his father did and his grandfather did—takes a special kind of masculine sensuality. Twenty years ago, he promised his father he would "never attend barber college." He didn't realize when he signed up to serve our country that he'd inherit the family business, even stationed thousands of miles from home, from the shop he grew up in. He talks to men all day. Unlike me, he knows how to talk sports: the Packers or the Lions, the Tigers, the Red Wings, or the military, or Korea, coffee, tattoos, or family, wives and daughters. The things men speak about in a place where men cut men's hair. He can pick a conversation topic out of the air and wrap it around the chair like a tarp. He makes conversation thin paper, and he wraps it around our throats.

He knows he's the one with the power, the one we trust to hold the razor to our necks, and pay him and tip him to do it. But he knows how to please his wife too. Sometimes he lets her win. He's the one who spins the chair, or he raises it up, or he changes the channel. He's the one who plays bootleg VHS tapes of men beating each other bloody, the ones he scored in Iraq. Or perhaps it just stays on Fox Sports forever. Either way, he isn't afraid to say I love you to another man, even in public.

I tip the man and leave the shop, but my heart still beats arrhythmically. I realize he wasn't speaking to me when he said "fag," but I still didn't defend myself during the microaggression. Five years later, when I chastise a stranger at an intersection for driving while talking on his cell phone, he'll call me faggot; the interaction will end with me screaming outside a CVS during Pride Month, "You should try getting fucked in the ass some time. You might like it." Today, however, I chose flight over fight, and I still wonder if it was right.

The October air chills my damp, aftershaved scalp. I'm late for my meeting; I won't have time to shower, so I brush my head off with my sleeve as best as I can. Still, the black hair trimmings stick into my skin. For the rest of the day, they'll itch down my back, on my shoulders, and through my shirt. They'll fall into my eyes when I sweat, and cling to my palms when I hang my head in my hands. They won't draw blood or kill me; they'll stab me in my neck and behind my ears like tiny spears.

ON

ALCOHOL

At the beginning of the pandemic, I start drinking dirty quarantinis: a heavy pour of New Amsterdam vodka—chilled from the freezer, bottle like an art deco quartz—a splash of white vermouth, two olives, and a dash of brine, maybe something fancy from the local farmers market like kimchi or pickled turnip brine if I've got it. It doesn't taste great, but it feels somehow luxurious, and the high proof means it hits hard and fast. I'd never order a martini at a bar, preferring beer or a simple mixed drink. When my roommate asks, How are you doing? I hear it more like a statement, perhaps an accusation. It sounds like, I noticed you drinking a lot of straight liquor in the middle of the day, and I'm worried about you. But drinking at home is in vogue. Bars are closed, local municipalities have legalized takeout cocktails, and breweries aren't even filling growlers. We're doing Zoom happy hours. And it's a stressful time to be alive; isn't it a little lovely to be numb? So I pour myself a second and we binge *Community* and believe we're flattening the curve.

I stock up on cranberry juice and V8, mixers with a long shelf life that go well with the liter-and-a-half bottle of vodka I decide I'll be keeping on hand while waiting for the virus to blow over. For variety, I grab a gallon jug of cheap fruit wine and a twelve-pack of a seasonal craft beer and stash them in the pantry for the next three weeks until I feel comfortable grocery shopping again. For the first few months of the pandemic, when the groceries come home, I let them sit on a shelf for three days before touching them; if I need them earlier, I'll wipe them down.

Have you ever done drugs or alcohol the first thing in the morning? my therapist asks.

It's our first session and we're both feeling each other out: he'll ask questions to assess me and my symptoms, while I'll decide if he'll be a good fit to help me manage those symptoms. I'd always been neurotic, but ever since the pandemic, I've reached a new level of anxiety, one that I feel slither across the skin of my arms and thighs, one that makes my shoulders shudder and shuts my brain down like its yanking out fuses. I'm having a hard time getting work done, I'll tell him, and the fall semester's approach feels like the rising tide and I'm worried I'll get swept beneath the surf.

Yes, I say, remembering pouring whisky or rum into my morning coffee before work or class, the bitter warmth creeping from my stomach to my brain. Something to spice up the bus ride or first half hour of a shift. I'm also no stranger to a morning beer or bloody Mary in an airport. It's easy to justify, it feels like time doesn't exist while waiting for a 10:30 a.m. flight. But I don't tell him this, I just say Yes, because it's only our intake session and I figure he's just asking for demographic purposes. If he wants to probe me about my specific vices later, I'll let him.

Thanks for your honesty, he says.

Yeah, of course. I've never struggled being vulnerable with therapists. At the end of today's session, when he asks me about my strengths, I'll list my own openness, how I wear my heart on my sleeve. How I'm liable to highlight my own flaws when I'm, say, on a date, or teaching. What else can I do when a lesson plan is imploding in front of my students but to laugh along with them and over-explain why things went wrong? There's something about calling attention to awkwardness that diffuses it.

Have you ever felt the need to cut down on your drinking? my therapist asks.

Yes, I say. I explain how I've quit drinking—twice, for six months at a time. Once in 2020, and once in 2021. I was drinking two drinks a day in the pandemic. Well, at least two, I clarify. It's nice to have a beer or two at night with dinner, but it's also easy to forget that's fifteen drinks a week, sixty a month, over seven hundred drinks a year. It's sinister math. In 2021, I moved to Barbados for six months to work from home in paradise, and the novelty of being abroad meant I started drinking again. Bajan rum punch: Barbados rum with lime and pineapple juice, bitters, and a grating of fresh nutmeg on top. Living alone on an island, it was easy to pick up a bottle or two of wine each week while grocery shopping. I'd mull it with star anise, cinnamon sticks, orange slices, maple syrup, so it felt fancier than drinking a ten-dollar bottle alone. Besides, once the bottle is open, you have to drink it soon, or else it'll go bad. That's what I'd read online. So it makes sense to have two glasses a night.

But I quit again after that.

Why? he asks.

Well, it's a lot of empty calories, I say. I've lost a lot of weight, I've gained some of it back. When I was counting calories, I made sure to budget for beer. Plus, I tell him, it has some bad interactions with medication, like painkillers and SSRIs, so it's just easier to skip it altogether.

■

When a nurse prescribes me Prozac over the phone in 2020, I don't take it. I'd been staying up watching news for sixteen hours a day: Facebook livestreams of protests, endless images of police in body armor lobbing tear gas canisters at teachers and mothers, unmarked vehicles whisking citizens away in Portland, Proud Boys armed with baseball bats prowling Boston. I was staying up all night, sleeping for four hours, and waking at 11:00 a.m. to coffee and more bad news. The nurse also prescribes an antipsychotic after I tell him it feels like a civil war is coming. I never take that either. It's hard to believe him after he suggests George Floyd was responsible for his own murder.

Where do you think it will take place? the nurse asks.

The cities, I tell him. The streets. It already sort of is. There are militias out there who don't like people like me. They're already training with weapons and shields. Today. They're doing military-style drills and formations. They're ready to bash skulls and we won't be prepared.

What would the two sides be? he asks, and I feel his skepticism through the phone. I remember stumbling through an answer like, The left and the right, and I'm afraid the police might side with the right.

Three months after our conversation, the FBI will arrest thirteen men for conspiracy to kidnap and harm the governor of Michigan. In 2022, two of them will get charged. That same summer, police in Idaho will arrest a couple dozen people in masks with shields after intelligence tips them off. They rent a U-Haul to hide out in to allegedly disrupt a Pride event there. A video of men handcuffed with zip ties surfaces on Twitter. They're kneeling in the grass on the side of the road wearing face coverings, gaiters and aviator sunglasses, and

On Alcohol

jackets with phrases like "Reclaim America" and "Conquerors, not Thieves." They believe they have a right to stolen land. A journalist identifies them as members of a group called Patriot Front. It's shocking to know there are groups of men who hate men like me. It's equally shocking that police actually apprehended them.

The nurse and I plan a six-month follow-up appointment. By then, I'd be in Barbados, using a VPN to spoof my digital location so I can continue to receive health care abroad. I toast the new year with prosecco and local starfruit. I don't take the antipsychotic because I don't trust the nurse; I don't take the Prozac for a couple reasons—maybe the scariest part is that it will change me. But maybe being unchanged is worse. By incredible kismet, the follow-up appointment is scheduled for January 6, 2021, and I ask the nurse if he's watching the news. From an island nation, I've got on NBC's YouTube livestream, and as I watch MAGA rioters spray bear spray at D.C. police and beat a cop within an inch of their life with a flagpole during the attempted insurrection, I can't help but tell him, I told you so.

■

I've only blacked out from drinking twice, both times in college. Once at a house party, where I arrived late, and played catch-up shooting bottom-shelf tequila chased with Minute Maid lemonade, a putrid combination. I'd end up walking home, which I don't remember. What I do remember is waking up at my kitchen table with my laptop open and a nonsense message mashed into Facebook Messenger. The other time was at karaoke, which must have been the third or fourth bar of the night. I have vague memories of drinking a thirty-two-ounce sex on the pool table out of a Big Gulp-style plastic cup at the city's diveiest bar, a syrupy cocktail of melon Midori, blueberry or peach schnapps, vodka, pineapple juice, orange juice, and Curaçao the size of a small fishbowl. There's lots of variations, but what matters is it's liquor and it tastes good. We scream through a rendition of "Creep" by Radiohead in a Lynchian bar with red walls and cheap red carpet, and when I get home, I stumble quietly in the dark and fall over and hit my head on the nightstand. The next morning, I skip class and my mom takes me out to breakfast, where I have to hide out for a few minutes in the bathroom in case I end up vomiting, looking at pictures on my camera roll I don't remember taking.

■

Thanks again for your honesty, my therapist says. Have your friends or family ever been worried about your drinking or talked to you about it?

No, I say, and it's the truth.

The reason I'm here, though, I tell him, is plain old anxiety and depression.

A few months into social distancing, I have a dream where I'm in a car with someone— perhaps a stranger turned lover— and neither of us are wearing a mask, and my skin bristles at the thought. When I wake up, I fix a drink, then write a poem about it. About the dream, and about the drink, vodka cranberry. This is the first time I remember *feeling* anxiety on my skin. This is the seed of my physiological symptoms—a dream about a fear of being touched in the pandemic. And the feeling is worrying. Sometimes, it's a flash of skin-on-fire. Other times, it's like someone crashed a pair of cymbals in my ear and I'm jumping. It's like my blood is flinching, I tell him. It feels like I'm always waiting for the other shoe to drop.

My therapist nods but doesn't write anything down as I try to metaphorize my physiological symptoms. Another therapist before him offered up a logical, scientific answer: cortisol, a stress hormone responsible for, among other things, the fight-or-flight response. And as thankful as I am for something—a noun, a neurotransmitter—to attach these feelings to, it doesn't stop the symptoms or make them any easier to deal with.

I tell him, At this point, I'm not sure if I'll ever eliminate anxiety, or if I'll just be managing symptoms.

Well, he says, in my experience, probably managing symptoms.

Thank *you* for your honesty, I tell him, smiling behind a KN95 mask, and his eyes crinkle too, acknowledging the joke.

∎

The pub and grill in Michigan doesn't pay well, but it doesn't pay terribly either. On Fridays, I trim whitefish in a basement and prep for the evening fish fry rush. What's nice, though, is we get a free drink for each shift, a double if you work full time. Doesn't matter if you're in for four hours or fifty minutes, Jim says, take your shot. Or beer. Any shift over five hours gets you two drinks, he explains at orientation. Lots of us take American Honey, sometimes tequila with lime. Occasionally I'll stay for a beer instead.

The pub serves pints, but customers can upgrade to a thirty-ounce glass goblet of craft on draft, a local cream or honey ale, an IPA if you can stomach it. At 9:00 p.m. on Fridays, for surviving the rush, everyone working gets a celebration shot of liquor, and another at midnight if you're still on, to toast the new day. The midnight shot is every day, not just Fridays, Jim clarifies. Rumors circulate that a manager has been sneaking extra shots in the back room. I'm almost certain it's true, but he stays on staff because he still works hard. It's almost impossible not to drink on the job. I get home tipsy after an eight-hour shift and have a shower beer while I wash fryer oil off myself.

In California, we have a faculty get-together at a distillery. I get there early with my friends and we eat hard cheese and prosciutto, and try their homemade gin with tonic, plus a lemon drop. Before long, others have arrived, and I chat with coworkers and their spouses. Some of them were left homeless by the fire in November, but we try to move through that bit of the conversation, since everyone is sick of having it. I have three drinks and a water, then another, and I know I'm still a little buzzed, but a break in the conversation feels like a natural time to say my goodbyes. Someone asks if I'm good and I say yes.

I use Google Maps to direct me home in the dark, relying on the voice speaking directions, but the turn comes up fast, and rather than miss it, I choose to take the turn. Sharp. I feel the momentum of the car yank me sideways inside the cab. I think I remember the sound of wheels on cement as I brake too hard, too fast. I think I remember another pair of headlights. Somehow, I correct the vehicle and don't hit anything or anyone.

On Alcohol

At home, I fix myself an old fashioned to calm my nerves; I eyeball an ounce or two of Bulleit bourbon, add a dash of bitters, a splash of water, a maraschino cherry, plus sweetener. I don't keep sugar in the house, so I use real maple syrup. The cocktail is one of those numb-your-mouth strong drinks, which I like. I can imagine the eighty-proof bourbon seeping into my mucus membrane, into my cheeks, and under my tongue. Sometimes beer just doesn't cut it. It's all carbs and carbonation, no buzz.

When I quit drinking the first time, I start drinking mocktails. I buy fresh mint, limes, lime-flavored seltzer, grapefruit, cucumber, and a three pack of alcohol-free spirits, large bottles of still water infused with spices and herbs that add a little bite. More than the flavor, though, there's something about the ritual. I cook up some simple syrup, muddle the herbs and fruit with the back of a wooden spoon, measure the spirits, slice the lime, toss ice into a mason jar to use as a makeshift cocktail shaker. Once it's cold and frothy, I strain it into a nice glass and top it with seltzer or fruit soda. The fake tequila is smoky and peppery, the fake citrus liqueur smells exactly like Cointreau, and they make a great mock margarita.

It feels good to have quit drinking and it feels good to tell people I've stopped drinking. I post a few pictures on Instagram, so for a few months, sobriety is a part of my brand. It's not difficult to abstain, but I do still feel a pang walking past a liquor store or corner store.

White Claw has a new hard seltzer. It's 8 percent, twice as strong as their original recipe, for only a dollar more. Plus no empty calories, no unnecessary sugar or juices. I go through a twelve-pack a week. When I feel like I've been showing up too often at the liquor store—when they start to recognize me, nod at me when I walk in each Saturday—I find a new liquor store. Just to mix it up. Just so it doesn't seem like I'm drinking too much. Sometimes I'll get a fifth of rum and a bottle of Caffeine Free Diet Coke instead. All the calories come from the ethanol, not the mixer, so it's better for my health, I tell myself. I don't like drinking caffeine too late, and if my plan is a few rum and Cokes at home in the evening, I don't want it to affect my sleep.

■

Alcohol affects my sleep. A couple friends and I hit the bars in Minneapolis; my friend Joey is in town, so we hit the Saloon, then Up-Down. I only have five drinks, which is the medical definition of a binge, but I drink them over five hours. A cider. A beer. Two rums with Coke. Plus some cocktail from Claire that the bar messed up. Joey rarely drinks, but it's a special occasion, his first gay bar, and he catches his first real buzz off two White Russians. Five drinks feels manageable. Joey and I Uber home and eat leftover Pizza Lucé, but I only get about four hours of sleep before the liquor wakes me up.

I know I'm hungover from the feeling in my throat and my gut and my eyes. It's 5:00 a.m. and I can't fall back asleep, so I lie with a blanket over my eyes and try to keep the light out, and try to keep myself from vomiting through force of will. I breathe steady and measured through my nose.

On Alcohol

Then I start sweating. For three hours, I lie on my back with sweat dripping down my forehead and into my ears, pooling on my sheets, leaving a cold stain in the shape of my body. I've pickled myself, my fingers pruning in my own brine. I worry that if I stand, I'll puke, a feeling which rests in my diaphragm.

I hear Joey wake up on my couch and start watching Netflix, and I know when I leave my bedroom it'll be to use the toilet. I turn on my Bluetooth speaker and play the new Beyoncé album to keep him from hearing my heaves, and when we start our day, I can only eat three bites of my McDonald's. I leave it to get cold in the car, then finish it a few hours later.

In high school, my parents offer to buy us booze, as long as we drink it in the house. We're not party teens, so we only try it once. I have a double rum with orange juice and it's the first time I feel a buzz, the warm sleepy loopy dizzy feeling soaking behind my eyes while I grind some levels in RuneScape. Besides that, I never drink in high school. In fact, I identify as "straight edge" for at least a year into college—a person who foregoes any alcohol or drugs. I even had a hoodie with a straight edge logo: an arrow inside a circle pointing up, signaling that you're "above the influence." I hadn't accepted my own homosexuality, and I feared losing control. I knew drugs would loosen my lips and I'd confess. Or maybe I wouldn't even speak, I'd just grab the nearest boy and kiss him. And then everyone would know.

I think one reason I'd avoided drugs and alcohol for so

long was that fear of accidentally coming out. I wonder if every queer kid fears this. You're three drinks into the night, or stoned for the first time, and you forget to code switch. Any drug could be the truth serum that might out you. You say "he" when you meant to say "she" and it'd be mortifying. Life-ending. In the 1950s, the US experimented with dosing citizens with LSD as a truth serum as part of a program called MKUltra. Between 1953 and 1973, the CIA tested LSD as a tool for interrogation and brainwashing. The CIA would secretly dose men in San Francisco brothels, as well as mental patients and prostitutes—"people who could not fight back," according to officers after the program was declassified.

These days, my mom rarely drinks, but my stepdad will have a Miller Lite with dinner, plus keeps a liter and a half of Seagram's 7 Crown blended whisky for mixing with soda. Just to have on hand. When I'm home for Christmas, mom will buy me a six-pack of craft beer, but sometimes I'll take a shot from the whisky bottle if I need something harder, something to numb my mouth and put me to sleep.

■

I teach my students about reliable sources. When I was in high school, I learned that .edu, .org, and .gov websites tend to be more reliable. But any organization can buy a .org domain. That includes neo-Nazi organization StormFront, as my English teacher demonstrated during our sophomore year, showing us how they'd infiltrated the top Google search results for "martin luther king jr."

Another .org is 4chan and its offshoots, an early 2000s imageboard that spawned dozens of classic Internet memes, but which also fuels alt-right ideologies, transphobic and antisemitic conspiracy theories that occasionally crystalize and escape into the mainstream. They, too, are interested in MKUltra, blaming the rise of American school shootings on it, rather than on gun culture and racist replacement theories. To them, mass shootings are either false flags or the result of a new CIA mass feminization drug plot. It's not uncommon for 4channers to erroneously make the leap from a photo of a shooter with long hair dyed blue to leftism to transness, to shift blame onto vulnerable minorities. Or even spread misinformation intentionally, trolling that the killer must have been one of those gender-questioning Bernie bros and using photos of two different people as their evidence to sow confusion. These users are either ignorant or malicious, and I'm sure they say the same thing about me.

He's a radical liberal, this will disappear from news outlets in 3...2...1, wrote one Twitter user about the twenty-two-year-old Highland Park shooter, despite the shooter's Facebook profile containing photos of the shooter at a Trump rally, wearing Trump gear, wrapped in a Trump flag, and attending anti-mask trucker rallies.

See the rose on his neck? wrote another, posting a photo of the shooter's tattooed face. That's DSA, that's antifa.

Gotta admire the @FBI, wrote a third, when not framing black people for fake drug crimes, they seem to always find 115 pound white guys with mental issues for their latest false flags. He'll tweet: Alex Jones was right about Sandy Hook. He is being made an example by the Deep State.

A .gov website can also be biased, I tell my students. The DEA classifies cannabis, as well as psychedelics like LSD and mushrooms, as Schedule I, meaning no medicinal use—contrary to most scientific knowledge—and heavy chance for addiction. This places them in the most dangerous category, worse than other drugs with recognized medicinal use such as cocaine, ketamine, Xanax, Vicodin, meth, oxycontin, Adderall, and fentanyl.

Alcohol is not scheduled.

It's hard to believe that pot outranks drugs with multiple confirmed annual fatalities and serious, long-term side effects like fentanyl, coke, and ketamine. But then again, perhaps it's not really that hard to believe at all, given the history of racist medical practices, the prison-industrial complex, and the CIA's alleged trafficking of crack cocaine in communities of color.

■

At the end of our first session, my therapist looks up from his notepad, into my eyes.

This is my last question, and it's my favorite, he says.

Uh oh, I say, embedded in a nervous chuckle.

What are your biggest strengths?

Well, I say. I'm smart and funny. I care, a lot. I think I'm open and honest.

I noticed you didn't say you're a good writer, he says.

I noticed too.

I'm creative, I say instead, which maybe is a way to sidestep having to say I'm a good writer. It's getting harder to believe that spending hours at a keyboard researching, obsessing, composing, revising, and writing an essay that might never get published or pay me anything or be seen by anyone other than a few academics even if it does get published is something I want to do. I used to believe in writing, its power, but lately everything slow—like writing—feels much less urgent.

I have a lot of doubts about my future, my ability, my discipline. About the ability to get paid to write, or to consider it my career. Or whether that's even what I want to do. Doubts about the impact of my writing, or lack thereof. And I'm anxious about that feeling too—if I'm so unsure about writing, why even do it? Things in this nation have been on fire, and I'm not sure writing attaches to a hydrant big enough to stop the blaze. Maybe I am good at writing, but in which ways does that actually matter?

And then I remember I'm supposed to be listing positive things, not self-doubts. And anyway, it's time to pause the session.

He asks, Does this time next week work for you?

∎

It's been hard to live substance free and it's been hard to trust the state, so there's times when I don't do either. The CDC's response to the pandemic felt at once sluggish and not enough, and it turns out the surgeon general's March 2020 messaging (read: tweet) against buying masks was based on supply-chain issues, not health standards. Police murder and lie and beat protestors on camera until they lose eyes; they go on paid leave, then they transfer stations, or they don't. They push an old man onto the concrete in Buffalo, cracking open his head; they escort fascists into the Capitol. A controversial reality star who lost his presidential reelection campaign appointed three Supreme Court justices, who each lied about their intentions to overturn *Roe v. Wade*. And after decades of mass shootings, the needle on gun control hasn't budged.

And when the Supreme Court rules in favor of gay marriage in 2015, the conservative newspaper at my future MFA program will lie too. In an article titled Gay Marriage Ruling Sparks New Era of Totalitarianism, they'll write: "Laws are no longer reflective of what the people 'do' want, but what they 'should' want."

They'll claim that there was no mandate. They'll write:

> They could have won their rights fairly, but instead took an unconstitutional victory at the resentment of the entire nation. They could have received national legalization in a constitutional manner, but were instead used as puppets for the acquisition of federal power. What laws the future has in store remains unseen, but it is apparent that the nation's consent will no longer play a role.

And in a way, they're right: seven years later, the Supreme Court is now a supermajority Republican and abortion is no longer a guaranteed right in the U.S.

It feels like things are crumbling while my conservative neighbors cheer it on. And I'm sure they feel the same about liberals. I breathe steady and measured through my nose.

■

At my first tarot card reading, my friend asks for a coin.

On Alcohol

I know this is kind of weird, they say, but I need a token, something worth value, then it needs to be discarded, it'll be used up. I hand them a quarter out of the change jar, shuffle, and pull: the Devil, Three of Cups reversed, Four of Cups reversed. The Devil means there may be a moment in the future where you find yourself struggling with addiction to drugs, maybe alcohol. The Three of Cups reversal here means you'll want to face this struggle alone rather than with the support of others. But remember your Four of Cups reversal, they say, tossing the spent coin into the kitchen garbage, You don't always have to look inward. Don't forget your friends will still be there when it's over.

When they leave, I think hard about pulling the quarter from the bin.

■

I get together with friends at a brewery each Wednesday to play board games and drink beer. I tell them I'm sticking to one tonight, and sometimes I do and they join me. But sometimes the second drink is too tempting, the allure of a numb buzz too seductive. Sometimes when 5:00 p.m. rolls around and I feel the call, I'll flip a coin, asking it whether I should pick up a six-pack for the weekend. Sometimes I listen to the coin. Other times, I choose for myself.

■

I'd like to think I'll quit drinking for good one day, maybe soon, I tell my therapist at our second session. I want to imagine a sober future.

I just don't know which day it will begin.

M—,

How do I begin this? Do I say I tried writing an essay about you once but it felt flat? You already know that. Do I wonder on the page whether words can capture friendship? Or has that story already been told? Does this become an essay about how I used to believe writing could do anything, until I realized it's just a facsimile version of speech? A rotten tool like a rusted hammer with a splintering handle? Just something we get by with? How we do things with our mouths and bodies when speaking that could never translate to prose, and yet—

Before I get ahead of myself, I guess I can start at the beginning.

We must have met playing *Magic: The Gathering.* I can't say for sure, but that's how I met lots of our friends around that time. At its core, it's a fantasy trading card game about arithmetic, skill and luck. I've been calling it a combination of chess and poker, a game where chance matters, as do—as turns go on—previous game actions. You like to speculate on the collectible market, I like to collect, and we both like playing the game. Some of my earliest memories of you: me, venturing across the quad to your dorm's lobby to trade cards and play a few multiplayer games with you and the other *Magic* players in your hall. Facebook says we became friends in December 2013; you'd have been turning twenty-two on New Year's Eve (People always count down and cheer when my birthday is over, you joked), and I'd be twenty-three the following month. But my memory wants to place us further back than that. Maybe we met at our college's anime club, when you were twenty and about to move out of the dorms, and I was twenty-one and just starting out on my own, writing my first rent checks and learning how whiskey makes my head feel like I'm underwater.

We would have been sitting at West Hall, the one notorious for its artsy, bohemian student body. You were there to study math, but you still looked the part of a college artist: long, dark brown hair feathered back, not even a little contained by a wool cap, a purple off-brand hoodie and a goatee. You looked like Shaggy from *Scooby Doo*, shuffling a handful of cards at the community gaming table in the lobby. You got that a lot back then, "You look like Shaggy." You still might.

I remember showing up with Joey and his binder full of rare cards from his high school days, and I remember this caught your attention. These cards hadn't been reprinted in half a decade and the new competitive gameplay mode allowed players to use their older cards, so although their supply stayed the same, demand was going up. Joey didn't play the new style, so he traded you his old stuff for your new cards. You saw it as an investment, and we saw it as an upgrade. It was a fair trade, financially; as time went on, their price charts would weave and dip. These days, both cards have been reprinted enough that their values have more or less evened out. Time has a way of flattening things out.

I can't remember our first conversation; if I did, perhaps I'd write a scene here where I say, I'm John, and you'd say, Hey, I'm M—, and then I'd write our bodies doing actions. But that feels flat too. What I can say is, like me, you were drawn to the absurd. Once, while on the phone with your mother, her cat got into some pizza boxes on her kitchen counter, and you championed the cat. Mom, let that cat have some

M—

pizza, you told her over the phone, and I laughed so hard and cheered alongside you. Or; I'd tell cashiers, Oh, that's the year I was born, no matter the total, $19.44 or $17.74, waiting for the cashier to catch on to the joke. I remember when you dyed your hair one shade of brown darker and waited for us to notice. I think that's absurd too; you went from brown to dark brown. Jack said something right away. I never would have noticed.

In pictures of us from that time, you wear a graphic tee with a Godzilla vomiting a rainbow. I would have been in neon blue plaid or maybe a T-shirt that referenced a 90s show like *Rugrats* or *Legends of the Hidden Temple*. Did you know that stuff's back in style again? You wouldn't believe how many Nickelodeon hoodies I've seen on the bus here in Minneapolis this year alone, seems like one every day. Later, you'd adopt a more neutral look, opting for striped sweaters and dark tones, but you held onto purple. When I was writing this, and scouring your social media for pictures from the last decade, I was surprised to see you dyed your hair aquamarine in 2010. In my mind, you're so utilitarian, but then again I guess you've always been a bit flamboyant too, trying on makeup and various pieces of "women's" clothes you'd thrifted.

Yes, I tried writing an essay about you in grad school. I wrote in some cheap, decorative details, like how, in conversation, you pretended to pick lint off your sock. I thought it was expected and generic, something I could have written about anyone to feign familiarity. But when you read the essay, you liked that detail. I wanted to capture your essence on the page. I thought it felt hollow and expected, but you thought I'd nailed it. In the essay, of course, you're playing *Magic*, and I hone in on your play style, how you'd rather count the opponent's life total down from twenty in increments of one rather than large chunks of four or five, aligning with a more "bleed them out" play style. How you seemed to love incremental advantages in your own life as well: charging everything to a credit card to get 2 percent cash back, then paying it off before the interest kicks in, or how you always brought a sandwich to class rather than overspend at the sub shop next door. How you seemed to never stop doing math in your head, your impeccable mental ledger, the credits and debits. You were both the cheapest and richest person I knew, thrifting all your clothes and driving me home in winter in your beat-up van, the heat coming on at the tail end of our twenty-minute commute, because you'd loaned your '90s Subaru with hand-crank windows to your dad, because you traded cars every other year, because he lived with you, partly because he couldn't afford to live on his own, and maybe also wasn't stable enough, but perhaps also wanted the company.

I still tell people all the time, you're "my friend who paid off his economics degree by selling *Magic* cards and *World of Warcraft* items online, by flipping Lego on his online store." I always envied your financial prowess. My mother jokes that I inherited her financial ignorance, how neither of us know how a 401(k) works, the difference between mutual funds and index funds. You taught me what a Roth IRA was. Probably two or three times. I still don't have one.

Did we ever live together? Maybe for a summer or my first year of grad school, at that house on Spruce Street where the basement stairs were so steep, we had to unscrew the handrail to get our TV down there? Did you spend a few months in that upstairs room by the washer-dryer? Or was that someone else? Sometimes it's hard to pick apart

M—

the memories. So many houses, so many addresses and permutations of roommates. Sometimes I imagine life like a ship in a sea; details get lost in the salty spray and they crust over when the waves stop.

Actually, I forgot Jack wasn't even living with me when I finally moved out of the house on Everett. I forgot he moved in with his girlfriend in 2017. Can you believe I forgot? In 2022, we were in Colorado, catching up in his car for the first time since the pandemic, and he said, That was back when I was living with Riley, and I said, Who? He said, Riley, my girlfriend? Ooh, of course. They dated for years; somehow the memory had left me. We sat down in his condo to smoke weed and play a game of *Magic* together for the first time in four years and he said the cutest thing. He said, I've dreamt of this moment.

God, that puts a stupid smile on my face just remembering it. And the feeling is so good—and these days, so foreign—that it makes me want to cry. It just undoes me.

At some point you had an open invitation to our house. I'd come home to find you on our couch playing *Overwatch* on the living room PlayStation, drinking a Labatt Blue. An import, I liked to joke, even though it's true. Even when you bought your own house three blocks down, you still made yourself at home at our place, and we welcomed you. I imagined you going home—back to your place, I mean, because you were at home at our house too—and sliding into your computer chair in the dark, lit by your dual monitor setup, with your automated *RuneScape* item mining bot on one screen, stocks and Reddit on another, and your father hasn't had the energy to bathe in days, and you spend a quiet evening watching the numbers go up.

You know, you're one of the reasons I learned to cook. I remember sitting at an Applebee's, you'd ordered wings and I, the quesadilla. It was late enough for half-off appetizers, which was the only time we went, so we could afford twice as many. We hated the kitschy sports memorabilia on the walls, but we liked six-dollar brew pub pretzels.

Why'd you get the quesadilla? you said.

Because I wanted a quesadilla. Why'd you get the wings?

Because I can't make them at home. I don't think I'd ever pay twelve dollars for a tortilla and cheese, it's so easy to make. But I'm not frying my own hot wings, you said, dunking a drumstick in ranch.

And that was that, but it planted a spore in my brain that changed the way I think. Somehow I'd reached college without learning how to cook anything besides instant ramen and frozen pizza. I'd grown up on prepackaged food and my parents' cooking, but my siblings and I never made an effort to help out around the kitchen. I wonder if I even owned a cutting board back then. Surely, I had a dull, awful knife and beat-up pans with flaking Teflon. But from that moment on, I started seeing the kinds of foods I could make at home on every menu: wraps, salads, sandwiches, eggs and toast, and bacon. It seems silly now, but your frugality rubbed off on me that day in a Midwestern Applebee's. I got more adventurous in the kitchen, assembling stir-frys and sauces, salmon with veggies, roasts with potatoes, and beans and rice. Pretty soon I had a couple dozen recipes I could call to mind. And sure, I didn't save enough for a mortgage when I stopped buying avocado toast, but it must have saved me thousands of dollars over the years. I grew to love feeding you and our friends from my slow cooker: chili with cornbread, yellow curry with shredded chicken, pulled pork with coleslaw on brioche. It felt good to nourish you.

You don't believe me when I tell you I have an angry streak. You didn't know me then. Once a kid called me "King Kong" because I was fat and Black and I punched him in the face. Once in high school, I threw a bowl of soup at a kid for teasing me. I got into lots of fights in school; I got detention and suspensions when I lashed out. I didn't know how to control my emotions, especially when I felt slighted, teased, or embarrassed. To me, it was self-defense. I felt like a loser, but I wonder if kids perceived me as a bully. Maybe more like a bear not to prod. Sometimes people would come to me after and say, Yeah, that guy deserved it. And I can't blame you for not believing; it's a part of me I've had to keep down.

The weekend of the wildfire, I was driving with my coworker and her daughter through Berkeley and a guy cut me off; I laid on the horn for a full minute until he finally parked in the middle of the road and got out of his car to yell at me through my rolled-up window. I stared straight ahead until he stopped. Do you know how long one minute is? Do you believe me now? We'd planned to stay in the daughter's college dorm, to wait out the smoke from the Camp Fire, which would turn out to be the deadliest and most destructive in the state's history, but I was so embarrassed by my own road rage that I dropped them off at the dorm, told them I couldn't stay, and drove two and a half hours back home toward the smoke, crying into my N95.

The first time we did acid, I bought it. Despite living straight edge for two decades, I think I always knew I'd try it. It was a bucket list thing. I brought over three Altoids with the drug pipetted onto it, wrapped in tin foil. I showed you and Jack the mints under black light, how the LSD glowed fluorescent; they looked like tiny white cupcakes with radioactive neon icing. We planned an activity day: coloring books, bubble wands, a movie, some albums to listen to, *Magic* if we needed something familiar. We wanted to be childish. We swallowed them down and waited. We felt nothing but the menthol. We played *Magic*. At one point I thought maybe the letters on my phone were moving around. I think I saw them wiggle, I said. That was it.

So we did it again. This time, I bought tabs, white cardstock with a haphazard grid drawn in pencil by a dealer, so we knew where to cut it. We took two, each barely the size of a pupil. Then I threw a slab of meat into the slow cooker and we waited for the drug to take us. We felt it first in our stomachs, the way it feels to climb a roller coaster, that same tickle of excitement.

Lance drove us to a mountain and we climbed it. At the top, lying on my back on the hot rock, I stared into the blue sky through plastic sunglasses and watched a thin white grid spiderweb softly across it. We let the sun warm our dark hair and tan our skin. In *The Snow Leopard*, Peter Matthiessen describes an acid trip, where he discusses feeling connected by invisible roots to his wife, and when I read that book later that year, I'll remember this moment where I'd felt the same thing with you; it was like I could read your mind. The way your body and face turned, I could almost hear you say, We should head down soon. Then you said, We should head down soon. Maybe there's some scientific explanation behind it, how psychedelics enhance the ability to read body language, and maybe that resembles a psychic experience. Maybe I don't want science to explain it.

M—

Is it cliché to say tripping puts you on a certain wavelength? That everything feels like an inside joke, that people-watching can entertain for hours? That the cyclical nature of time feels so much more pronounced? Before I know it, the kids playing on a rock down below are former versions of myself and my brother, or maybe their father is a future version of myself, and I wonder if you see it too, you and your brother in those boys. And I wonder how many men have looked at boys and seen the simultaneous past and future. And then I'm thinking about gut flora, the way bacteria inhabit us. And our planet is a microbe that we inhabit. And if it's a speck of dust on the black sleeve of space, what are we? A speck within a speck? And there's something freeing in that.

Is this the place to experiment with form? To write an essay whose presence on the page somehow resembles, mimics, or mirrors hallucinogenic drug use? To utilize a structure— or design my own—to elevate this prose? Does the essay discussing itself simulate the headspace of a psychedelic experience? Or will it always be facsimile?

Or, does it make sense, here, to reach for the lyrical? To describe how wood grain flowed and dripped like poured honey? It did. Or how bricks in the façade breathed, or how the ceiling fan seemed to pulse translucent concentric circles from its center like an icy aurora, or the warm sultry notes of Lance's guitar as we came down in my living room, or how the natural glow of light anointed everything that day? Some other pseudo-religious metaphor? Should I say that, when we stayed awake until daybreak, it wasn't just a morning, but the dawn of a new life?

How many times do you think we've tripped? How many supposed dawns of a new life? Ten? Twelve? More? I asked

Jack and he said six, but you know how his memory is. I can count more than ten distinct times. Does it matter? This essay can collapse any number of them into a singular experience, like how stars fall into their own gravity and become dense black holes. Is there a craft choice that suggests a supernova?

Remember how mad my roommate got? How she didn't want us taking pills or tabs, only mushrooms and other "natural stuff?" How we feigned sobriety on New Year's—your birthday? Or maybe she never found out. We shrugged it off at the time, but she had a point. I watched an episode of *Dateline* with my mom where a high school girl died from taking what she thought was LSD but was really a research chemical, a toxic NBOMe mislabeled by some dealer. That was always a risk, and I know you did enough Internet research to have known that. I'd known too. We stayed up until Lance came home and we wrapped ourselves in blankets, started a fire, and he looked into our dilated eyes and told us the story of his friends' Christmas party, tales of liquor and shrooms and Adderall. That year was so cold.

Once, you told me you enjoy looking up to people. As if it were one of your hobbies.

For example, I look to Jack for his fashion, you said. I find someone who does something better than me, and I make them my mark. I try to be like them. For fashion, Jack is my mark.

M—, you're my mark, I confess, and a goofy smile finds itself on my face. Did you know that? I ask. And my smile is catching because I can even see it now, in my memory, on your downturned face.

There's so many things about you I admire, I said. How you aren't afraid of money like I am. How you protect your

M—

own time. How utilitarian you are, how practically you think. How you aren't afraid to wear eyeliner or high heels or carry a purse. How you don't call it a "man purse." Your analytical mind. How you see the world. How you value things, how you assess risk. Then we rode our bikes back to my place and ate pulled pork.

During one part of your mania, you'd start drinking at noon each day, having beers at the brewery down the street and writing in your notebook, then staying up well into the night, traveling to different dive bars, offering cigarettes, making new friends each night, people I'd never know. You still came over every few days, but you started to have a life outside our tight friend group too. Maybe you felt yourself expanding with nowhere to go. Or maybe you worried you were too much for us and had to ration us. M—, you weren't too much.

I've been tracking my alcohol use on a calendar, you tell us, weeks later. You'd turned away a Labatt Blue I'd offered from my fridge. Surprising: we always keep a thirty-pack on hand and it'd been your turn to buy. Life's been a big party for the last few weeks, you say. Fourteen drinks last week. I think it's good to take some time off. That's another one of those things you said that still sticks with me; last month I wrote an essay and I quoted your logic, the idea of counting weekly drinks. It's one of your habits I can't stop. Your voice still sounds in my head.

We fought about money once. I was sure you made more than any of us at your salaried IT position, probably, what, sixty grand a year? Eighty? So when you complained about splitting beer money, and accused us of drinking faster on weeks when it was your turn to buy, I pulled up my mobile banking on my phone and shoved it into your face. This is my net worth, I told you. I showed you how much I had in checking and savings, how it summed to just over four digits. Actually, subtract twenty-five thousand in debt. I bet you make my entire net worth in a week, I said. Jesus Christ, M—, you're probably the richest person we know. I'm a grad student. If I miss two paychecks, I'm done for. Can you just buy the next round? Please?

It was stupid and childish. Twenty-something-year-old men—boys—bitching about beer money. It was twenty-two bucks a week. Split four ways. And it wasn't your fault that I was in debt (and still am). I was sick of you complaining about money, and you had so much. I just wanted you to shut up and pay it. You saw an unnecessary expense. We were both right. I guess part of the reason you became the richest person I knew was your frugality. You once told me the richest people look the poorest. Someone who buys a sports car is flaunting new wealth; someone who drives a beat up Geo from the '90s is the sign of someone who scrimps and saves. I can't remember who bought the next beers.

I hadn't minded buying my share of beer, or even extras, on weeks when I knew I had more cash to spare. I get that from my parents. Each year, they splurge on snacks and meals for the family cottage; I'm writing this from a cabin where I brought groceries to share with my MFA cohort: fair-trade bananas, local salsa, tortilla chips, organic hummus, a jar of peanut butter, a carton of oat milk, the expensive brand of granola, baby carrots, a bag of tangerines, a loaf of bread, a carton of eggs, a jar of mayo, a bottle of mustard. I'm not expecting anything in return. My parents are the first to offer to pay at dinners. They'd fed my friends well into

M—

college. One year, they hosted a dozen of my dormmates for Thanksgiving. It all comes out in the wash, they say. They don't tally who owes what, and I try not to either. I bought them dinner the day I'd planned to come out to them with the first paycheck from my first teaching job, and the time felt right, if not belated; I was twenty-three, had never dated, and I thought it would be easier to tell them after nachos and a large margarita, but I waited until they were driving me home, and I told them from the back seat of their car. Really? my dad asked, though I'm sure they already knew. I never doubted that they'd love me regardless; I know you know I didn't need to make a quick escape. I guess I was scared of myself. In some ways, that hasn't changed.

God, remember the time you invited me to the bar with your friends and I ended up naked in front of you? You'd invited me to the bar to meet some of your new friends, and I recognized them both from Grindr, two guys older than us, one in his thirties and one in his forties. We drank beers and took shots and then went to the forty-something's home downtown. He showed us around his place, and I stubbed my toe on his glass table in the dark, and we all ended up in the bedroom, shirtless, massaging each other. I'd realized I'd left my wallet at the bar, so your friend ran (literally—ran, on foot) to get it while I straddled the forty-year-old's ass through our jeans and massaged his bare back, and he pressed up and back against me. When your friend got back, you massaged him too. Then, you stepped out for a minute, probably to use the restroom, and in that time, they'd asked if it was alright to take my pants down to my knees, and I steeled myself for you to come back into the room and see me supine with his head in my crotch. You stayed clothed, I kissed your friend, then they fucked each other. You provided their condom. I didn't come, not even close; I froze up and laid on my back until they finished, then I pulled my pants back up. I didn't know how to move my body; it was like watching the whole scene from outside the room, through a frozen window. Of course I was self-conscious. But if there was any desire in that moment, I was too seized to act. I don't know what you thought about the whole situation. I didn't know if you were gay, bi, pan, fluid, or just supportive, an orgy cheerleader. And I didn't mean to write about sex, but you're my only friend who has seen me nude. I can't even get changed in locker rooms; I get shy and sweaty, being perceived.

Did you know, I went back to his house once after that? After we saw each other on that dating app again. He was already in bed when I got there, so I stripped and laid next to him, and we dozed off to a bad Sci-Fi Channel movie and I said, What do you wanna do, and he said, Whatever you want, so we got each other off with just our hands, and I spent the night swaddled in his four-post bed with fluffy throw blankets, and his dog slept between us, and in the morning he offered me fat-free strawberry yogurt and dropped me off at home. Did he tell you that? Did word get around?

You know, I haven't slept with anyone since the pandemic. Jack laughed when I told him that. That's . . . a long time, he said. I know, I said, even though once every two years is average for me.

You know, in California, there was one guy. His hook-up had canceled on him so we got tea together. He was in town from St. Louis to clean up, three months after the fire. He thought he'd be out in the field hacking charred logs but instead they had him in the office, which he hated. He did

M—

charcoal drawings of serpents he posted to Instagram, and wrote music he didn't post to Instagram, and we talked for over an hour and drank warm tea, and it was quaint, and outside the tea house he turned and asked to kiss me, and he did kiss me, and the next day he came over and he said, I know we kissed yesterday but I feel like I fucked it up, can I kiss you again? and I said yes and he did and I loved the way he asked for consent and I took him to bed and when I said, Yeah, yeah, fuck me, he said I am, and I had never laughed during sex like that before, and he came over two other times before he had to leave town, and I spilled my guts to him in a text message five months later and he never responded, same as the last guy, and I guess I still think about him because I wrote a poem about him in grad school, and I'm back in grad school again writing about him now, but it's the only time sex has ever felt fun and I can't remember his name.

Except, when I was writing this, I searched my phone for "Grindr" and of the fourteen names there, I figured "Erik (Grindr)" was the one, and it is, and the last thing he ever said to me was, "That's the thing about fortune, we never know :) Speaking of which, how was your date the other night?" and before that, he said, "I'll gladly stay in touch and would like to see you in the future; but, AmeriCorps holds my leash for the next year of my life. Making long-terms plans isn't something I can do until then."

And the last thing I said was, "Hey Erik, I was just remembering what a nice time I had with you in January and wanted to drop a line and say I hope you're doing well wherever you ended up this summer," to which he never responded, and before that, I said, "Hey Erik, I hope you made it home safe," to which he never responded, and I remember how sometimes people lie just to be nice, and how embarrassing it is to put yourself out on a limb, and how the pleasure's never been worth the pain, and I guess what hurts the most is that I'd never felt so beautiful, and it's hard to imagine it happening again, but to him it meant nothing.

Things fall apart here. Maybe it's not useful to imagine a future different from the one I've built. Maybe I should let time flatten things rather than seek to dredge them up. I keep looking for a pattern of what I've done wrong, and my therapist tries to talk me away from that ledge. But I got ghosted again two weeks ago, and it's hard to believe I'm not somehow at least partly at fault.

I guess the thing that keeps me from identifying as asexual is the difference between "not experiencing desire" and "not desiring to act." Do I experience attraction? Yes, and so do other asexual people. Would I die happy never having anal again? Sure. Does that make me asexual? For a few months, I wasn't sure. It would take me another few years to discover the term "side," meaning someone who doesn't identify as a top nor bottom—not even as versatile—but as someone who prefers "outercourse" to penetrative sex. Coined in 2013 by Michigan-based sexologist Joe Kort—and finally added to Grindr in 2022—the concept of the side disrupts a binary. As much as gay couples love to joke about the logical fallacy that one must be "the woman" in a relationship, adhering to the established top-bottom dichotomy still falls into that same thought trap.

Sometimes I think pornography has poisoned my brain; I can let photos online remain fantasy without any mess—emotional, physical, spiritual, or otherwise. Yet, after the kissing scenes, I often fast-forward past penetration hoping to see porn actors participating in pillow talk. And I didn't

M—

mean to write "bro lit," but somehow this essay is about porn, drugs, and male friendship, your beat-up car and your relationship to your dad. I don't know, M—. I've slept with five people in ten years—only one more than once. There's people who have had more sex this week than I have, ever. It's not eating me up; really, I'm getting by. Maybe it's the Capricorn ice queen in me. Maybe the stars decided.

A few months after our botched foursome, I'd wake up to find you still drinking at 9:00 a.m., filling notebooks with rambling writing about ancient pharaohs and Internet-connected spy bugs inside my smoke detectors.

I wrote about the sun god, you told me. There. And you pointed to the cat in the cat tree by the lamp. You were drunk and bleary.

Did you sleep? I asked.

The sun god doesn't sleep, you said.

Well, I think you should sleep, I said. And were you drinking all night?

I'll finish this one and be done, you said. And you were. You left, then I left for work.

You left the notebook behind. We didn't know if you did that on purpose. And I don't know if it violates your privacy, but while you were gone we flipped through it, your whirlwind of scribbling, the rambling, seemingly-random nonsense and non-sequitur footnotes from your mind. We looked through it because we were worried about you.

Not long after, you got completely naked in a break room at work, threw an office chair at the TV, and were tranquilized by EMTs. We visited you at the hospital. They had you lying in a bed, hooked up to monitors. In my memory, the whole room is gray, the sky is gray, you're gray, we're all wearing different shades of gray. On a screen, a gray line jumps and throbs, monitoring your heart.

I saw a man who was very small, you said.

Where? we asked you.

On the bike trail. He asked for money so I gave it to him. I think he had a gun.

You were mugged? We are trying to understand.

He was very small, you say. He just kept getting smaller. I gave him the money.

The doctor asks if we think you were on any drugs at the time, and we answer honestly: no. You still hadn't slept, but you said you liked the view, how the moon hung over the architecture. You spoke to it all night. I picture you bathed in gray moonlight watching patterns change on the walls, the gray sound of hospital machinery. Far away, beyond your door: hushed, gray voices.

We visit you in the psychiatric hospital too. You're in there for a week and a half, and Jack and I must have stopped by two or three times. You aren't happy—how could you be?— but you understand why you're there, and in a way I think you're thankful for it. Later, you'd explain to me how something had compelled you to strip and throw furniture at the workplace TV over and over until your coworkers called emergency services, something about not being able to express your need for help in any other way, like the outburst was some sort of tool for you. Like your breakdown seemed inevitable. You tell me you want to write, but they don't let you have a pen in case you harm yourself or others. But you like the reliable bedtimes and mealtimes, making art, and reminders to stretch. You tell me the lithium makes you feel like a zombie. Although it's nice to feel more stable, you miss *you*. It will take time and patience to find the right kind of

M—

medicine that feels less like lobotomy.

Research suggests that, while psychedelic drugs likely don't cause personality disorders directly, they could trigger something latent inside us, causing things like schizophrenia and bipolar disorder to bubble to the surface earlier than if we'd gone without. Chances are, your symptoms are genetic; your father also struggles with intermittent periods of depression and mania. There's also a nonzero chance I handed you a drug that lit the spark. That's another one of your words I keep close: nonzero. According to the law of large numbers, anything with a nonzero chance of happening will happen, eventually, given enough time and a wide enough sample size. You told me that. British mathematician John Edensor Littlewood defined a "miracle" as anything with a "one in a million" chance of happening; he calculated that each of us experiences a "miracle" once a month, which is one of those things I'm sure you understood intuitively, but which I needed the religious metaphor to comprehend.

So I suppose I'll end like this:

M—, it's good to see you, I said. We were sipping beers at the brewery down the street from your place before the new year. When did they add this room?

They bought the property next door last year and expanded. It's nice. Then we both admired it. Then you said, How's everything? and before I could answer, you said, You know my ex? She moved back in. We're still broken up but we're sleeping together too.

I see, I say. And how do you feel about that? fearing I sound too much like your therapist.

It is what it is, you say, sounding like me. And I kicked my dad out.

Oh, you did? but it's not a question. Where is he now?

I dunno, you say. Somewhere in Wisconsin. Back home.

I'm sure it's better for you, but it's late December and it's hard to think of him unhoused, though I don't tell you that. Instead, I tell you about the wildfires in California, how smoke blanketed the region for three weeks, how you couldn't escape it even if you drove three hours to the ocean, how the smoke wasn't just from burnt trees but from everything in people's homes—burnt rubber and Lysol and Lysol bottles and propane and laminated photos, and pets: dogs, cats, chickens, horses—and how it left students and faculty homeless over Thanksgiving break. How firefighters used our school as a staging ground to keep the blaze at bay, and how the building smelled like smoke for weeks after because of it. How burn scars lined the drive.

And that's the last time we've seen each other. Later that month they would find that spot in my mother's breast; I'm sure you heard. Yeah, she's alright, just a few complications after her double mastectomy, just one unplanned wound-care surgery, just a couple side effects from the chemo and chemo pills, but she checks in every day, and we Zoom once a week. I know what you're thinking: it couldn't have happened to a nicer person, and I agree. I was in town in August (I'm sorry I didn't stop by); I drove her three hours to Green Bay to have her latest round of stitches out. After a fifteen-minute appointment, I drove her three hours back home, and I tried to play music that wasn't too sad on the ride back, and napped for hours when we got home.

A funny thing about getting older is how you start to see people from your past in strangers. At the risk of sounding saccharine, I'm reminded of the line from *The Shape of Water*,

M—

adapted from a poem by Hakim Sanai: "Unable to perceive the shape of you, I find you all around me. Your presence fills my eyes with your love. It humbles my heart, for you are everywhere." Last week I saw a sweater that reminded me of you. Today I saw a TikTok of a person with features so similar to yours, I kept pausing the video until I found a frame where they looked just like you. I've seen people here in town who look, from the right angle, just like you, the illusion is so real. But what would M— be doing in Loring Park? It wouldn't make sense. Still, the mirage whips me back in time like a Proustian madeleine, and for a moment it's easy to believe it could be you, that you'd hopped a plane to the Twin Cities for a weekend, booked a room at the Millennium, boarded a bus and spent a lazy Tuesday window-shopping for holiday gifts downtown.

And I know I don't look like a lot of people back home, but I'm sure you've seen me too: on campus, at Walmart, at restaurants that no longer exist. On your travels (are you traveling much?). Knelt over tying my shoe, until—they turn, and the slant of their nose or brow isn't quite right, and I'm sure you feel that pang, realizing the impossibility of me there or then.

All this to say: don't drink too much, and I'll try to do the same. Say hi to your dad if you see him, and I'll say hi to my mom.

And I'll be home for Christmas, and I'm sure I'll see you soon,

John

AN

UNSTABLE

CONTAINER

On a July afternoon in 1828, Flag Lieutenant Robert FitzRoy, the twenty-three-year-old son of English aristocrats, stood aboard the deck of the HMS *Beagle* alongside Captain Pringle Stokes. After nearly two years at sea together, and surviving through a bitter winter navigating the Straits of Magellan, the men shared a sigh, staring into the sapphire saltwater of the Tierra del Fuego archipelago. The South American hillsides were verdant and alive, the mountains capped with snow. But while FitzRoy saw the beginning of a long adventure, he could never know what Stokes saw: two more long years at sea, no way back to his home in Surrey, in southern England. No escape. Stokes had agreed to captain the *Beagle* on its first voyage; however, when the journey proved treacherous and desolate and lonely, Stokes fell into a depression.

That night, Stokes closed the door to his captain's cabin and locked it. By mid-morning, he'd still not emerged. FitzRoy was surprised when Stokes missed breakfast. Together, the crew worried. After navigating through the archipelago that morning, FitzRoy headed below deck. Crouching, he descended the dark and lamplit hallway to find the captain's door still locked. He knocked. No answer. He tried again and no answer. The lamps flickered like a fading pulse. The crew was leaderless but experienced; they finished the day without him.

That evening, FitzRoy tried to rouse Stokes from his room again. He'd talked to onboard doctors; it was unlike Stokes to be seasick. He tried to talk with Stokes through the wooden door with no success. After several minutes, he gave up, retiring to his own room for the night, where he dreamed about a terrible storm, miles of clouded sky, the scent of expiring fish, the wind carving through albatross wings, lifting him up and out of the boat, and then back down and into the pillow of water below.

■

Mom baptized me Catholic, but only so Grandma wouldn't have a conniption. I don't remember this; I had no say in the matter. To this day, my mother is not a believer. But my grandmother's teachings howled in her ear. Unbaptized infants go to purgatory; if they grow to be unbaptized adults, they go to Hell. My dive into holy water was predestined. So Mom drove us to the nearest St. Peter's or St. Michael's and allowed the priest to hold my tiny body above a blessed font, to say the words he needed to say, to let the light from stained glass refract onto my new skin, and to bathe me in the waters he'd blessed himself.

Growing up, my parents never took me to church or Sunday school, never taught me scripture or verses or sins or forgiveness. My earliest knowledge of "my" religion came from after-school TV specials and from friends whose parents dragged them to church each week. Apparently, we were all created in seven days. Then there was a garden, a snake, an ark. We owe everything to a man who died for our sins, said my friends. Wasn't I friends with Jesus? I started telling kids at school I was Catholic; it helped me make friends.

My grandmother clung to the Catholic tradition under which she was raised. She had my mom when she was forty—the church strictly forbids birth control. Condoms go against God's plan; if he wanted you to have sex, it was for procreation, and a latex barrier interfered with this. Catholics believe the only two factors that determine your

An Unstable Container

eternal salvation are a quick dip in the baptismal font and the confession of every sin. In this way, I'm just one step—an apology or three-thousand—away from heaven. I've never been to confession—I wonder what the chasm between our definitions of "sin" looks like.

Our family celebrated Christmas and Easter, but I wouldn't learn the religious meaning behind holidays until much later. Christmas was never a birthday; Easter wasn't about Him rising from death. Instead, we celebrated the extra-long weekend, strings of sparkling lights. We celebrated glimmering ornaments, our sometimes-fake tree, my mother's cooking, turkey with trimmings, the earthy scent of celery and carrots cut for stuffing, my father serving ham and pineapple and pistachio JELL-O pudding. We celebrated my brother's fork shearing off a slice of canned cranberry sauce, my sister's spoon scooping mashed potatoes, the shared meal on the good china, plastic fake grass, rabbit-shaped chocolate, and sticky jelly beans. We held to these traditions. They weren't religious, but they were ours.

■

By late July, the *Beagle* had reached Port Famine on the north shore of the Straits of Magellan, and Stokes had spent two weeks locked inside his cabin by himself. FitzRoy had heard the whispers of mutiny, of someone taking the helm while the absent captain composed himself. He'd even heard rumor from one of the cooks that FitzRoy himself had been suggested as the new captain, his intuition solid and blood royal. But he shoved the idea from his mind. He had learned a lot about the ship in the two years spent sailing, but he didn't yet consider himself captain material. His focus had been hydrography—charting and taming the murky depths of the salty sea, the curves of shores and ocean floors, the way tides moved in and out each day like lungs. And besides, the ship still had a captain, and FitzRoy wouldn't dishonor the man whose lead had saved their lives a dozen times or more.

Still, any effort to speak to Stokes during those two weeks was met with silence. FitzRoy tried each day for the first six, then he stopped trying. The steward said he thought he'd seen someone Stokes's height in the kitchen late one night, but couldn't confirm it was him. The crew had grown used to life without a captain. They slept, woke, bathed, cooked, ate, sailed, sang, reckoned, slept, dreamed, sailed, loved, woke, slept, woke, worked without him. They never mutinied; they waited for their captain, but Stokes would never open the door.

On August 1, Stokes put his pocket pistol in his mouth and pulled the trigger. A lieutenant heard the shot and told the rest of the crew. With the help of the carpenters, they managed to pry open the door. Inside, they found Stokes bleeding out, a hole in the roof of his mouth. With the ball of lead still embedded in his skull, Stokes remained coherent for almost eleven days before succumbing to gangrene.

■

At ten years old, I convinced my mother and stepfather to take me to a Christmas Eve midnight Mass. Through my Catholic friends at school, I'd learned the true meaning of Christmas. It wasn't about buying the latest video game console; it was a birthday. Something about the idea of gathering in a holy

An Unstable Container

place appealed to me that night. The nice clothes, singing hymns, camaraderie, peace on Earth, the colorful stained glass, velvety red carpet and golden pews, the thin, crispy Bible pages I'd only ever flipped through at a family friend's funeral or a cousin's wedding. It might have been the first religious service I attended. We didn't own a Bible.

That night, my folks and I dressed in our Monday best: pinstripes, slacks, and smart flats. A couple of neckties for us boys. As supportive as they were, they must have been stumped at my spiritual rebirth. As a family, we set off to find a church, eyeing each fluorescent cross from car windows, Dad trying to determine which midnight service might finish the earliest. My mom suggested the nearest oratory.

We entered an unfamiliar church. I sat on the oak pew and opened the hymn book in front of me. I didn't know any of the songs, and when we had to stand and sing, I mouthed the words. My parents did too. Halfway through, my father's stomach grumbled; a woman in a large hat turned to glare. Together, we suffered the hour-long liturgy. The priest's words didn't impress me. In fact, I don't remember a single one. But I do remember the joy of stealing away for a minute, splashing around in a stone font filled with murky holy water and soggy dead leaf fragments and rotting maple samaras.

I've never talked to God. I do recall spending some number of nights as a child on my knees praying by my bed. I'd seen the maneuver in TV shows; to get what you want out of the Big Man, you've gotta clasp your hands and kneel by a bed. Orange streetlight strained through my dark bedroom window, and I put my forehead to my hands and mouthed the words I needed Him to hear. I never prayed for the safety of my family, but for new toys, or to get myself out of detention. I prayed for shorter school days and longer weekends. I prayed that we'd play dodgeball in gym tomorrow. They were greedy prayers. Sometimes, I tried whispering my prayer aloud, but I didn't know whether that worked. I held my hands so close to my forehead, closed my eyes so hard that luminescent auroras danced behind my eyelids, and I wished and wished so loudly to myself.

FitzRoy would oversee many modifications to the *Beagle* before its second voyage in 1831. He'd been selected as the new captain following Stokes's suicide, and had several specifications before taking the ship back in the ocean. He ordered the exterior copper refinished, polished and shining. He had the upper deck replanked, and even paid out of his own pocket to replace the iron cannons with brass, for more accurate surveying; the iron's invisible, magnetic tug interfered with sensitive equipment. He ordered the deck to be elevated eight inches to allow more headroom below, which some sailors reported even helped stabilize the ship while at sea.

As the second voyage grew closer, FitzRoy grew anxious; excited to sail again, especially with his new position, he knew he could avoid some mistakes Stokes had made. For one, he would make sure to include crewmembers who shared interests, so that everyone would have at least one person to talk to, to stave off loneliness. But FitzRoy also dreaded sharing the same room Stokes had had. He didn't believe in ghosts—he was a staunch Christian man and knew suicide meant Stokes's soul was damned in Hell—but to revisit the captain's cabin felt morbid, almost perverse. The blood had long been washed away, but FitzRoy wondered how much had soaked into the planks, how much still lingered in the air, and how much blood he might lose in that cabin himself on this voyage.

■

When I asked my father what he believed in, if he believed in God, he grumbled. The question must have thrown him off guard. I was maybe thirteen, riding in the passenger seat, perhaps on the way to buy mustard. We had never talked about God before. He had eschewed the sanctity of "'til death do us part," divorcing his first wife and marrying my mom when I was six. We moved in with him and his two children, my stepsiblings. In polite conversation, I drop the "step." I call him Dad because he is. We share no blood.

Sometimes we feel like we are two unsynchronized frequencies; he towers above me in height and in wavelength. He's closer to his own son, who, unlike me, would survive through Boy Scouts; who, unlike me, cared more about fishing and women than his classes. Both men are lanky with long limbs. Both reach six feet tall and prefer Miller Lite.

Dad exhales through his nose. "I don't really believe in one true God," he says after a beat, drumming his large hands on the steering wheel, eyes still on the road. "But I do believe in a force or a power or something out there. There's something out there," he says again, unblinking. Sometimes he felt like God, a force of mercy and salvation; he married a single mother. He raised me, a child who was not his own. He would send our family dogs to Heaven—sleeping pills in

American cheese, or a heavy blanket of carbon monoxide—the only times I've ever seen him cry.

■

I tried to give blood twice in high school, the first during a Halloween blood drive. I chose to donate because a poster featuring a vampire was clever. The blood donation process began in the gymnasium with a questionnaire. Anyone aged sixteen or older could donate, learn their blood type, and get fed apple juice and chocolate chip cookies.

"Just a few easy questions about your history," said the nurse after pricking my finger to check my iron, her features round and soft, her hair the color of cocoa. She and the team of nurses would pull blood from dozens of young bodies and stash it in specialized coolers, taking them back to the hospital twenty minutes east to be tested for further diseases, medications, or other disqualifying pollutants. The blood would be stored and used locally for transfusions.

The nurse handed me the questionnaire.

Are you feeling well today? Yes.

Are you currently taking any antibiotics? No.

Have you donated blood or plasma in the past six weeks? No.

Female donors: Are you pregnant? n/a

In the past 48 hours, have you:
Taken aspirin? No.
Had a cold? No.

In the past 8 weeks have you:
   Donated blood, plasma, or platelets? No.
   Received a vaccination? No.
   Been in contact with someone who has received the smallpox vaccination? I don't think so.

In the past 12 months have you:
   Had a blood transfusion? No.
   Come into contact with anyone else's blood? No.
   Had a tattoo? No.
   Had a piercing? No.

Have you ever:
   Been diagnosed with HIV/AIDS? No.
   Had malaria? No.
   Had hepatitis? No.
   Been to Africa? No.
   Been in sexual contact with someone from Africa? No.
   Used intravenous drugs? No.
   Male donors: have you ever had sexual contact with another male, even once? No.

I sat in the plush chair and surrendered my right arm to the nurse. "You have beautiful veins," she said, fingering the thin, sensitive skin. She stained my inner elbow pumpkin orange with iodine, probed for a vein, then drove the cold, hollow needle into my arm.

She handed me a stress ball. "Keep squeezing." My fingers curled and then loosened around the spongy toy, muscles contracting, tendons stretching and retracting while warm type O positive—"the universal donor"—filled a plastic collection bag. Soon, I fell into a rhythm. Squeeze.

Relax-squeeze. The room felt colder as the blood left my body. Once I'd filled the bag, the nurse withdrew the needle and bandaged the circular wound, but when I stood, I felt my blood pressure drop. The ambient voices from nurses and other students muffled out, and my vision reduced to a pinpoint.

"Wow, you're pretty pale," the nurse said, her voice echoing as if from some other reality. She sat me back in the chair and raised my legs above my heart so blood could drain back into my face. An aide brought my cookie, and I ate it slowly as the gymnasium blurred back into focus. Bleachers uncollapsed, faces reformed. Light reentered my pupils.

■

The August before embarking on the *Beagle*'s second voyage, FitzRoy asked a fellow hydrographer for advice about taking a travel companion with him. He knew the loneliness and isolation of the sea, and sought to travel with someone who shared his passion for science, who could use the voyage for research, who he could call a friend for the five-year journey. FitzRoy found a young Cambridge graduate student named Charles Darwin to fill the position.

Between September and October 1835 alongside Captain FitzRoy and the rest of the *Beagle* crew, Charles Darwin traveled to four different islands in the Galápagos: San Cristóbal, Floreana, Isabela and Santiago. Darwin noted that birds from different islands in the archipelago each had slightly different beak shapes, fifteen different beak shapes in total. This dimorphism, Darwin hypothesized, allowed the finches to gather food—to survive—on each particular

An Unstable Container

island. The finches with longer beaks would peck holes into a cactus fruit to eat the pulp inside, whereas the finches with shorter, more narrow beaks would tear the cactus to mush, consuming both the plant and any larvae inside, maximizing their feeding opportunities, and, thus, their survivability, especially when food was scarce.

Finches that were better equipped at finding food survived longer, had more offspring, and passed on similar traits. The traits that gave certain species an advantage over others would carry on from parent to offspring, and so on, changing one species of bird ever so slowly into another; this theory could explain the dimorphism across the islands. This same process gives oceanic single-cell organisms the ability to sense, to detect light through pinpoint eyes, to better find food, and eventually to become something different, to become multicellular, to grow, to advance, to develop legs and to escape the ocean. With enough time, this process turns primordial goo into humans.

Upon their return, FitzRoy wrote an account of the voyage but edited the notes taken during the *Beagle*'s voyages, claiming the notes contradicted "the authenticity of the Scripture"; the discovery of seashells in layers of sedimentary rock subverted his literal reading of the Bible, of Noah's ark and the six-day creation story. He erased the previous captains' logs, afraid that the misinformation would reach young sailors and poison their minds.

The Royal Geographic Society awarded Captain FitzRoy a gold medal for his findings.

I first learned about Darwin's finches in elementary school. By tenth grade, I'd taken a stake in science. I trusted it with the answers; prayer didn't work, but narrow finch beaks did. While natural selection provided an answer to how we got here, it said nothing about our current situation, why we're still here today. A biology course attempted and ultimately failed to answer that question for me. We started the unit about reproduction, "the natural process among organisms," said the textbook, "by which new individuals are generated and the species perpetuated. Every organism that exists is a result of reproduction."

As a closeted high schooler, I failed at selecting mates that biologists could consider "fertile," and I could never help perpetuate our species. Not long after that, I concluded: "I have no purpose." Why would a divine creator design a human who couldn't execute his chief biological purpose, his meaning of life? He wouldn't. After all, the God that I knew but perhaps didn't believe in makes no mistakes. Each body is crafted in His divine image. Yet, I still exist. Therefore, I concluded, God must not exist.

It's not a perfect logic; however, I reeled from the revelation. I didn't practice a religion, but I felt like repenting. I didn't believe in God, but I felt like someone had betrayed me, placing me onto this planet like a spare part. Functionless. Purposeless. What kind of god would put me here, and why? I couldn't find an answer, so I developed a self-loathing instead. Seeing couples laughing in restaurants or holding hands around the halls in school ignited jealousy in me. Why should they deserve to be happy when I can't possibly achieve the same thing? Can't they see how good they have it? How could anyone complain with a perfect life like theirs? They have a use. I do not. They can't know how lucky they are. I wish this part of the story had a happy ending; I do live each day with pride, but some days I still wake up wishing I were straight, that finding dates were easier, that California bakers couldn't take away my rights to buy a cake, that I could celebrate a pregnancy with my partner, and share blood with my future child.

FitzRoy would grow to resent his participation in the *Beagle*'s voyage. A staunch "flood geologist," he hoped their survey would have lent more credibility to Christianity's creation story, literal evidence of the biblical flood to help explain humanity's origins. In fact, he had inadvertently helped push along a controversial theory: that all species arise through natural selection, what biologist Thomas Huxley would coin as "Darwinism." The theory was observed through animals, but it included humans, and this conflicted with FitzRoy's understanding of the world and how we got here.

At first, Huxley had been a harsh critic of the theory of evolution himself, writing a negative review of Robert Chambers's 1844 publication *Vestiges of the Natural History of Creation*, which proposed an early version of Darwinism. However, Darwin would share his findings with Huxley before the publication of *On the Origin of Species*, a privilege shared by few, mainly Darwin's friends. Eventually, Darwin would convert Huxley. He started calling himself "Darwin's bulldog," defending the ideas presented in Darwin's book. Huxley would volunteer to publicly debate and advocate for Darwin's theory against nonbelievers, including other biologists as well as clergymen.

In 1860, nearly twenty-five years after Darwin's finches, Huxley would publicly debate Bishop Samuel Wilberforce, an event that drew in nearly one thousand attendees to the Oxford museum, beneath arches like pointed poplar leaves, its open floor a cloister. Hundreds of people hoping to see the spectacle had been turned away at the door. Also in attendance was Captain Robert FitzRoy, who intended to argue against Darwin's findings. Against his own findings. He brought along his Bible as his evidence.

"Are you proud," Bishop Wilberforce said during the debate, "to call your great-great-grandfather an ape? Or your great-great-grandmother? Was she an ape?" He smiled, having struck such a fatal blow. "Who here," he said, addressing the audience, "Who among you here would find jubilation in knowing their grandfather was a gorilla? Is it of no consequence to you?" Murmurs drifted through the crowd like fog. The audacious claim that humans were no better than animals—that we descended from ape grandparents— spat in the face of God.

Huxley stepped forward. "I would," he barked. "I would not be ashamed to know my origin—our origin—is from a monkey." The crowd's murmurs became a rolling boil at Huxley's exclamation. "I would, however," he said, raising a finger, "be ashamed to know my grandchildren would work so hard to obscure the truth." He pointed that finger at Wilberforce.

When FitzRoy took the stage, he brought his Bible; he raised the heavy book above his head, each thin page a banner. "If I had known what I know now," he said, "I would not have embarked on that journey. I would have never let Darwin on that ship." He slammed the Bible down on the podium. The crowd, unsure whether to cheer or gasp, did neither. Instead, a silence spilled over the room, and a ringing sounded in FitzRoy's ear.

After my second blood donation, the hospital sent me a letter. Both donations tested positive for antibodies to hepatitis B, so I should contact a hematologist immediately for further testing. Failing twice suggested more than a false positive. Records indicated I had never received the vaccination, but my admittance into public schools almost guaranteed that I had. The presence of antibodies suggested, then, that the virus had been inside me. Test after test came back positive, but my doctor said my lack of jaundiced skin and cirrhosis meant a false positive for sure.

"Either that," he said, "or you somehow contracted it, had flu-like symptoms for a week, and now you carry the disease. You might just be a carrier your whole life," he said, shuffling around some medical records. "You won't know for sure until your health begins to fail. You'll be an old man, sick or beginning a round of chemo, and it'll affect your liver, and you'll think back to the time when a blood doctor said this might happen."

Contemporary medicine can't give me an answer, so I'll wait. I'm blacklisted from donating blood, organs, or plasma, even despite the low, low odds that I really do have the virus in me. It's a safety measure, like barring any "men who have sex with men." I will never be a part of someone else's body. My blood will never save a life.

John LaPine

Researchers have sought biological "reasons" for queerness in human beings—they look to the measurable benefits of a queer population. The most compelling, for gay men, is the "gay uncle" hypothesis—humans who cannot have children serve a societal purpose, carrying an obligation to provide resources for future generations and the offspring of their relatives. There exists a correlation between homosexual behavior and number of older brothers; with each older brother a male has, he is over 33 percent more likely to be gay. Hormone levels in the womb change between births. This also correlates to handedness: the "older brothers" theory only affects right-handed individuals. In this way, gay men may act as a counterweight to an overabundance of males. A population can correct itself.

Queerness is biological. Research demonstrates a number of physiological differences between heterosexual and homosexual individuals. Researchers at the University of Chicago studied the chemical reactions and metabolic differences between Prozac in heterosexual and homosexual men, observing the anterior hypothalamus, a region critical for the expression of sexual behavior in male animals. This part of the brain is smaller in gay men. They found that the gay brain reacts differently to Prozac; the drug even activated areas of their brains not known to affect sexual behavior. These areas remained dormant in heterosexuals.

This subverts the idea that homosexuality is a choice. Yet some still believe that we make some conscious decision to stop dating people of the opposite gender, to lie with a

An Unstable Container

man as with a woman, which is "a detestable sin," according to the New Living Translation of the Bible, "disgusting" to God's Word Translation. To King James, I am "an abomination."

Somehow I take comfort in the thought. In the idea of a marked, measurable difference between queer folx and the heteronormative majority. Partially, it's the irrefutable evidence that being gay is not a choice. Another part of me is relieved to know that perhaps there *is* a reason I'm here. But I didn't need these cold figures and scientific suppositions to grant my life purpose. Simply following all one's biological indicators, like a bodily how-to manual, would hardly lead to a fulfilling life.

Instead, I relish in daily miracles. How good melted cheese tastes on sourdough. How pink flowers bloom outside my apartment each spring. How, some days, when I wake up, I roll over to find myself sharing a bed with a beautiful man. How, sometimes, he'll grab my hand and bring it to his chest like a plastic rosary. How he'll play with my fingers while we both consider falling back asleep.

Twenty-nine years after his now-famous voyage on the *Beagle* with Darwin, Captain Robert FitzRoy, like Captain Stokes, took his own life. He would do it with a razor, preferring the intimacy of his own hand's skin to the impersonal iron of pistol. He recalled Stokes's eleven-day delirium, how the medical crew struggled to keep the captain afloat. How he begged to die. How saving his life went against his commands. FitzRoy waited until no one was home.

FitzRoy had already failed at discounting the theory of evolution with which he adamantly disagreed. He wouldn't fail again. He wouldn't repeat another man's mistakes. He washed his hands at his bathroom sink, picked up the straight-edge and sliced a clean line. He watched rivulets of blood puddle in the porcelain. With a whistle of tinnitus in his ear, he thought he heard his wife open the door.

I hope one day to get married. But this is not the hope of all gay men. Some shun holy union because of its religious origin, preferring free love over assimilation into monogamy. Others strive for a union that closely mirrors heterosexual marriage: the traditional wedding with suits and liquor and cake. But marriage is more than the sheet of paper we sign. And it's more than societal convention, first dances, and best man speeches. Marriage means rights. When my partner is hospitalized, I want to visit him. When he dies, I want the law to acknowledge I was his spouse, that we spent our years, money, and lives together as one. I want us to be able to die as equals.

In my dreams, our wedding is traditionally unique. One of us might play the groom, standing in front of your family and mine in a tiny bingo hall, palms damp and wringing, nervous with energy. You will wear a suit, and our friend will play the pastor, her face pierced and head shaved. She will ordain herself online and write the words she wants us to hear, the right things to unite us. There are no sides at our wedding; my brother sits next to your aunt, my sister sits with your father. Our cousins are our cousins. One of us

An Unstable Container

will choose to play the bride, walk through the door dressed in white, make our families rise, your father all tears. The organ plays Diana Ross and Marvin Gaye. My nephew's the flower girl; your grandmother laughs as he tosses pink silk rose petals into the pews and onto your uncles' laps. And then we will begin.

Our pastor will look us each in our eyes and say the words she wrote. She will thank your parents and mine for gathering here today in this bingo hall. She'll say, Love is an ocean; it might swallow you down, or buoy you. Either way, love's all around you. It will fill the cracks between your fingers and toes. It will slide down your throat and balloon your lungs. You'll swallow love like love swallows you. Love, she'll say, looks like open water and tastes saline.

You will pray for rain that day because you love the sound on rooftops. Someone will hear your prayer, and the sky will open up at noon, and peals of thunder will break across downtown, and we'll take wedding photos soaking wet in the park. In the photos, you will smile and I will try to fake a frown. We'll plan a spot to hang the snapshots in our den.

At the reception, my brother is the maid of honor, my sister's the best man. The bridesmaids and groomsmen are a collection of our closest friends. At the table, we sit and eat potatoes and roast beef and asparagus and watch our cousins and aunts and uncles dance and eat and talk and meet. You and I will sit in soaking suits. They will strike their forks on champagne flutes, and, for them, we'll perform the kiss. In fact, we'll kiss all night. And when the music stops and forks stop clinking, we will stand and tell our friends, Thank you for attending our party. It means a lot that you are here, that you could make it, we'll say. You mean so much. You matter.

John LaPine

Please eat and drink something, and love each other. And dance. Fill yourselves with food and light. Be alive tonight.

Then you and I will try to find a quiet place alone. We will survey the party before us, and in the chaos of liquor and laughter, we will hold each other by our hips, and say, Look. Look what we've done together. Look what we made happen. This is only the beginning.

And then we will begin.

ACKNOWLEDGMENTS

Thank you to Kim Todd and my nonfiction workshop from the University of Minnesota MFA program (Edwin Banks, Sonia Beltz, Noel Haines, Sarah Sukardi, Amalia Tenuta, andJordan Young-Zabrocki) for your care and comments on "M—" and "On Alcohol."

Thank you to Matthew Gavin Frank, my thesis advisor at Northern Michigan University, for your care and encouragement with the original versions of "An Unstable Container" and "NSVs." I don't know if you remember, but during my thesis semester, you once told me, "This essay is really close, it just needs about eight more hours of revision," which, of course, *you were right about*, but which caused me some significant existential / capitalist dread (which maybe still lingers a bit today), because I was working full time doing hotel laundry, and the thought of doing eight hours of "extra labor" when "I won't even get paid for this, and no one but me or my thesis advisor will ever read it" made me sick. Well, I'm glad to say, I was wrong; I got paid for it, and someone else is reading it now!

And thank you to my therapist, my friends and my family, who all put up—too often—with me writing our most intimate interactions into my silly little poems and essays. Yes, I changed your names to protect the innocent. Much love.

An earlier version of "An Unstable Container" originally appeared in *Under the Gum Tree.*

ABOUT THE AUTHOR

JOHN LAPINE is a Black biracial queer poet living & teaching in the Twin Cities. He earned his MA from Northern Michigan University in 2017, and his MFA from University of Minnesota—Twin Cities in 2024. His work has appeared in *The Rising Phoenix Review*, *Hot Metal Bridge*, *The /Temz/ Review*, *Glass: A Journal of Poetry*, *Under the Gum Tree*, *Rhythm & Bones*, *Midwestern Gothic*, *Underblong*, & elsewhere.